Liberal Democracy and Globalisation

*Compiled and edited by Graham Watson MEP
and Katharine Durrant*

Published by Bagehot Publishing

Liberal Democracy and Globalisation
Compiled and edited by Graham Watson MEP
and Katharine Durrant

ISBN 0-9545745-2-4

Published in December 2005 by:
Bagehot Publishing
Bagehot's Foundry
Beard's Yard
Langport
Somerset TA10 9PS

Printed by:
Contract Printing
1 St James Road
St James Industrial Estate
Corby
Northants NN18 8AL

Previous books by Graham Watson:

The Liberals in the North-South Dialogue (ed.)
FNS, Bonn 1980

To the Power of Ten - essays from the European Parliament (ed.)
CfR, London 2000

2020 Vision - Liberalism & Globalisation (ed.)
CfR, London 2001

Liberal Language - speeches & essays 1998-2003
Bagehot Publishing, 2003

EU've got mail! - Liberal Letters from the European Parliament
Bagehot Publishing, 2004

Contents

[1] The three MEPs representing Denmark's Venstre Party co-authored a common text.

Foreword

This is the fifth book I have compiled within five years. 'To the power of ten', '2020 vision', 'Liberal Language' and 'EU've got mail!' were all put together, as was this, during a hectic political career which allows insufficient time for a thorough and disciplined approach. No doubt they have all suffered. Nonetheless I believe it important to publish because politics is so ephemeral. Issues come and go, political alliances are forged and dissolved, our perceptions change - often imperceptibly. If I succeed only as a chronicler it is nonetheless an achievement of which I am proud.

'2020 Vision' was my first attempt at a collection of essays outlining Liberal Democrats' view of globalisation. It was published on the first of September 2001. The events of ten days later changed the world; so my book was outdated before it hit the bookshelves. I hope - for humankind as much as for the contributors to this volume - that no similar fate befalls this attempt.

I am indeed grateful to the eleven men and eleven women from the parliamentary group I lead for their contributions to this work. They have been gracious in the face of my exhortations and tolerant of my demands. Their chapters make good reading alone; in combination with others they provide a comprehensive insight into Liberal ideas about the world we inhabit early in the third Christian millennium.

Compiling and editing such a collection of essays comes inevitably at the cost of other priorities. Those who suffer most from my attempts to leave on the bookshelves of friends and sympathetic libraries some part of my life are my wife and children, since inevitably holidays are a victim. I thank them for their indulgence.

This volume would not have been possible without the patient editing and administrative skills of Katharine Durrant, who has helped me put it together on schedule for launch in January 2006. Her attention to detail, friendly advice and persistent but polite badgering of contributors have been invaluable. The other members of staff of my private offices in Langport and in Brussels have also lent a hand in various ways.

To all those who have assisted, I am grateful. I hope my readers' enjoyment is adequate reward for their efforts.

Graham Watson
December 2005

About Graham Watson MEP

Graham Watson was elected to the European Parliament in 1994 after a 15 year career which spanned government, private sector and freelance professional positions.

In Parliament he has served on the Economic and Monetary Affairs Committee, the Budgets Committee and the Justice and Home Affairs Committee. He was Chairman of the latter from 1999 to 2001. In January 2002 Graham was elected leader of the now 105-strong Alliance of Liberals and Democrats for Europe.

Graham's publications include 'To the Power of Ten: UK Liberal Democrats in the European Parliament' (2000), '2020 Vision: Liberalisation and Globalisation' (2001), Liberal Language (2003) and 'EU've got mail!' (2004).

His hobbies and leisure interests include sailing and listening to jazz music. Graham lives with his wife and two young children in the small market town of Langport, Somerset.

About Katharine Durrant

Katharine Durrant was born in Yeovil, Somerset and grew up in the South West, attending Wadham Community School and Sixth Form

College in Crewkerne. She gained a Bachelor of Arts honours degree in Modern History from the University of Nottingham and a Post Graduate Diploma in Law from Nottingham Law School.

Following her time at Law School Katharine returned to the South West, working for a regional law firm before taking up her current position as Research Assistant and Caseworker to Graham Watson MEP. Katharine is a Scout Leader and Guider with local units and enjoys hiking, reading and listening to music in her spare time.

Notes on the Contributors

Alfonso Andria MEP

Alfonso Andria is currently a member of the Committee on Regional Development and of the Committee of Environment, Food Safety and Public Health in the European Parliament as well as a member of the Delegation for relations with the United States of America and of several Intergroups. A law graduate, Alfonso is a member of La Margherita party and has been part of the Salerno Municipal Council between 1985 and 1993 and President of the Province of Salerno from 1995 to 2004.

Other previous posts he has held include member of the Bureau of the UPI - Union of the Italian Provinces (1995-1999), former regional Vice-Chairman of the AICCRE, and Chairman of the Federal Council of the League of Local Authorities (2001-2004).

Alfonso was nominated in 2002 as a Knight of the Order of St Gregory the Great and Knight of the Sacred Military Constantinian Order of St George.

Emma Bonino MEP

Emma Bonino is one of the leaders of the Transnational Radical Party and was a member of the Italian Chamber of Deputies for 18 years, until 1994. She has been a Member of the European Parliament for four terms: 1979, 1984, 1999 and 2004. She was appointed as a European Commissioner in 1994 where she was responsible for Consumer Policy, Fisheries and the European Community Humanitarian Office (ECHO) and later for Consumer Health Protection and Food Safety.

Emma's political activities are characterised by Mahatma Gandhi's practice of 'active non-violence' which is practiced by the Transnational Radical Party. Political campaigns launched by her party have involved hunger and thirst strikes, as well as acts of civil disobedience. Strongly committed against all forms of discrimination, her campaigns aim to 'regulate' and 'legalise' government measures. Emma is convinced that this approach is important in curbing criminal interests and overcoming dangerous gaps between society, laws and institutions.

Living in Cairo since July 2001, Emma has gained a deeper understanding of the Arab world. Her campaigns have included ratification of the Rome Statute on the International Criminal Court; promotion of women's rights (in particular the fight against female genital mutilation), advocating democracy, human rights and the rule of law in Arab and Muslim countries, and the start of accession negotiations with Turkey. In September 2005, she headed the European Union's Election Observation Monitoring in Afghanistan as its Chief Observer. Emma sits on the Committee on Foreign Affairs,Committee on Budget and Subcommittee on Human Rights. She is also an International Crisis Group Board member and Visiting Professor at the American University of Cairo.

 Maria Carlshamre MEP

Graduating from university in 1979, Maria Carlshamre went on to lecture philosophy in Gothenburg between 1979 and 1988. She also holds a Diploma in journalism (1988-1990). She has also worked as the Editor of TV 4 (1992-1995); written for the journal 'Moderna tider' (1996-1997), was a documentary producer for TV 4 (1998-2002) and Political Editor for Dagens Nyheter between 2002 and 2003. In 1996 Maria won the Swedish grand prize for journalism.

Elected to the European Parliament in 2004, Maria is a member of the Swedish Liberal Party and sits on the Committee on Civil Liberties, Justice and Home Affairs and the Committee on Women's Rights and Gender Equality.

Jean-Marie Cavada MEP

Jean-Marie Cavada has always been interested in international and European politics, starting out as an eminent journalist. He started his career in Strasbourg in the 1960s at Radio France Lorraine and Alsace, where he followed the work of the Parliamentary Assembly, the predecessor of the European Parliament. He later became the Chief News Editor at a succession of radio and television companies (including France Inter, Antenne 2, RTL, FR3 and TF1 between 1974 and 1982).

In 1987 he created, produced and presented the successful current affairs programme, *La Marche du Siècle*. In 1994, he founded and presided over La Cinquième, now the education channel of the France Television Group. After having been the President of Radio France Overseas (1997-1998), he became President of the Radio France Group (1998-2004).

Over the past decade Jean-Marie has also been a governor of the ENA (National College of Administration, 1993-1995) and AFP (The French Press Agency, 1998-2001). Returned as a French MEP in June 2004, Jean-Marie is now the Chairman of the Committee on Civil Liberties, Justice and Home Affairs as well as the President of the Press Intergroup of the European Parliament.

Marielle de Sarnez MEP

Marielle de Sarnez sits on the Committee on Culture and Education and is a member of the European Parliament Delegation for relations with South Africa.

Her past appointments have included Special Advisor in the office of Jean-Claude Gaudin, Chairman of the UDF Group in the National Assembly (1986-1988), Secretary-General of the opposition general assembly (1989-1993), Advisor to François Bayrou, Minister for Education, Higher Education and Research, then head of his office

(1993-1997), Secretary-General of the UDF Group in the National Assembly (1997-1998), Executive Vice-President of the UDF (since 2005), Secretary-General of the European Democratic Party (since 2004), Member of the Paris Council (for the 14th arrondissement) (since 2001) and Member of the European Parliament (since 1999).

Marielle has been the Chairwoman of the UDF delegation in the European Parliament since 2004.

Antonio Di Pietro MEP

After graduating from University in Rome in 1968, Antonio Di Pietro became a civil servant in Aeronautical Construction for the Minister of Defence where he was responsible for supervising armaments production. In 1978 he took first class honours in Law at the 'Statale' University in Milan, following which he specialised in Administrative Law at Pavia University.

Amongst other positions Antonio has been the town clerk in Pigra, Blessagno and Introbbio, near Como, and a Police Superintendent. In 1980 he qualified as a solicitor, and the following year embarked on a traineeship period at the Magistrature High Council in Rome and at the Milan Court of Appeal. After this he was appointed Deputy Public Prosecutor at the Bergamo Public Prosecutor's Office, specialising in organised crime, computer crimes and in crimes against public administration.

In 1989 Antonio was appointed to the post of Information Consultant by the Ministry of Justice. He initiated the 'Clean Hands' enquiry which investigated a long series of crimes committed by public officials and managers. In May 1996 he was appointed Minister of Public Works, and delegate to urban areas, Rome and Jubilee 2000, in the Prodi government. Elected as Senator in 1997, two years later he was returned as an elected Member of the European Parliament in the North West, North East and South constituencies. Returned for a second time in

2004, Antonio is now a member of the Committee on Legal Affairs and a substitute member of the Committee on Citizens' Freedom and Rights as well as chairing the European Parliament Delegation for relations with South Africa.

Mojca Drčar Murko

Mojca Drčar Murko graduated from the Law School of the University of Ljubljana and went on to gain a Masters in International Law and International Relations at the Law School in Zagreb.

While still a student she began work at the national radio station in Ljubljana, where she continued to work for the next ten years. By the beginning of the seventies, she was publishing articles and analysing international political events for Slovenian newspapers. After briefly working with the Faculty of Social Sciences, she became a foreign correspondent for the biggest newspaper DELO, assigned first to Bonn (from 1978 to1982), later to Rome (from 1989 to 1993), and finally to Vienna (from 1997 to 2003).

As President of the Press Council from 1984 to 1986, she contributed to the development of the Code of Conduct for journalists. Consequently a group of colleagues nominated her as their candidate for the (indirect) presidential elections in 1988 in the then Yugoslav federal state Slovenia. The irregularities of the elections excited public attention, eventually helping to bring about the first direct presidential elections in Slovenia (still a part of Yugoslavia) a year later.

After Slovenian independence in 1991, she devoted herself to writing about the legal foundations of the new state, international politics, the status of Slovenian minorities in neighbouring states and above all the integration of Slovenia into European Union. In 2004 she was returned as an MEP for the Liberal Democratic Party of Slovenia in the first elections to the European Parliament.

Photo: European Parliament

Antoine Duquesne MEP

After gaining his doctorate in law, Antoine Duquesne became an assistant lecturer in the Faculty of Law, University of Liège (1965-1971). He also practised law at Liège between 1965 and 1975. Antoine then went on to become Deputy Secretary-General for the National Committee for Training and Further Training in Trade and Commerce (1975-1977) and then took on the role of general administrator at the National Committee for Coordination and Dialogue on Continuing Education for Small Businesses and the French-Speaking Institute for Continuing Training for Small Businesses (1977-1982). In 1983 he became the Director of the National Fund for Professional Credit and has also been Head of Office to numerous state secretaries and ministers during the period 1973-1987. He was also administrator of several public institutions and is the author of a number of academic publications.

He was a Member of the Belgian Federal Parliament (1991-1999), Quaestor and Vice President of the Lower House (Chambre des Représentants) and Senator (1988-1991 and 2003-2004). He was the Minister of Education (1987-1988), Minister for Home Affairs (1999-2003) and Minister of State (from 1998). Antoine holds the distinctions of Officer, Commander and Grand Officer of the Order of Leopold and Grand Officer of the Order of Orange-Nassau.

Antoine was elected to the European Parliament in 2004, where he is a member of the Committee on Civil Liberties, Justice and Home Affairs and Vice-President of the Delegation for relations with Mercosur.

Lena Ek MEP

Photo: Magnus Fond

Lena Ek is a Swedish Centerparty and Alliance of Liberals and Democrats for Europe (ALDE) Member of the European Parliament.

Before her election to the European Parliament, Lena was a lecturer and researcher in Public and International Law at Lund University, in Umeå, and at the Raoul Wallenberg Institute.

Her political responsibilities and positions previously held include; member of the board for Södra Skogsägarna, member of the board for Valdermarsvik Municipality and Chairwoman of the Swedish Centerparty Women's Organisation, as well having been elected to the Swedish Parliament and being a member of the Centerparty Executive Committee.

Since her election to the European Parliament in 2004 Lena has taken on the role of coordinating the examination of energy taxation and emission permits. She is coordinator for the ITRE Committee and Rapporteur on the REACH (Registration Evaluation and Authorisation of Chemicals) proposals.

Jelko Kacin MEP

Jelko Kacin spent most of his life in Kranj, graduating from the Faculty of Social Sciences of the University of Ljubljana in 1981. He later became Deputy Minister of Defence during Slovenia's first democratic government.

He became known to the general public through his commentaries on the Gulf War in 1991 and in expert circles as a writer on defence matters. His special area of interest is aviation and air defence. Immediately before the ten-day war in Slovenia he was appointed Minister of Information. During the Slovenian War of Independence he successfully promoted Slovenia's demand for independence both at home and abroad. In 1992 he stood as a candidate in the presidential elections.

In 1994 Jelko was appointed Minister of Defence. At the 2000 general election he was re-elected to the National Assembly. In 2003 he was appointed to be a parliamentary representative to the European Convention and observer to the European Parliament.

Since 2004 Jelko Kacin has been a Member of the European Parliament and a representative of the Liberal Democrats of Slovenia (LDS). In October 2005 he was elected President of the LDS. Jelko Kacin is member of the Committee on Foreign Affairs, Vice-Chairman of the Delegation to the EU-Moldova Parliamentary Cooperation Committee, part of the Delegations for relations with Iran, with the Korean Peninsula, and the countries of South East Europe.

Silvana Koch-Mehrin MEP

Silvana Koch-Mehrin is a Member of the European Parliament, where she represents and leads the Free Democrats Party (FDP) of Germany. Since 1999, she has chaired the FDP foreign group Europe and is a member of the FDP Federal Executive. She also serves as Vice-Chair of the Group of the Alliance of Liberals and Democrats for Europe.

She is the youngest of the European leaders of major parties and is responsible for bringing her party back into the European Parliament after a ten year absence. Previously, she was a co-founder and managing director of a public affairs consultancy focusing on strategy planning and European issues. She has lectured MBA students on Business Communication at the United Business Institute in Brussels. She also holds an MA in Economics and History and a PhD in Historical Monetary Unions from the University of Heidelberg.

Baroness Sarah Ludford MEP

Baroness Sarah Ludford MEP has been a member of the UK House of Lords since 1997 and London's Liberal Democrat Euro-MP since 1999. She is a graduate of the London School of Economics, with a master's degree in European Studies, and is qualified as a barrister. Her career has spanned the UK civil service, the European Commission and the financial services industry.

She is European justice spokeswoman for the British Liberal Democrats in the European Parliament on the Civil Liberties, Justice & Home Affairs committee. This covers asylum and immigration, freedom and non-discrimination, and security and law enforcement. She is also a member of the European Parliament's Economic and Monetary Affairs Committee and its delegation to the Balkans. Sarah campaigns actively on a variety of equality, human rights and international issues: she is active in the Parliament's 'intergroups' on anti-racism & diversity (Vice-President) and gay & lesbian rights, a member of the council of Liberty and Justice and a patron of Fair Trials Abroad and the Guantanamo Human Rights Commission.

Jules Maaten MEP

Jules Maaten was first elected as a member of the European Parliament in the 1999 European elections. He currently sits on the Committee on the Environment, Public Health and Food Safety and the Committee on Economic and Monetary Affairs. Until June 2004 he sat on the Foreign Affairs Committee. He has done legislative work on such issues as the Tobacco Directive, the introduction of the euro, water quality, AIDS, safety of children's toys, car exhaust emissions, food safety, paediatric medicines and Dutch prisoners in Thailand.

Jules is part of the parliamentary delegation maintaining relations with the ASEAN countries and Korea, of the EU-Russia delegation and of a number of parliamentary intergroups including Consumer Affairs and

Animal Welfare. He has been active on EU foreign policy issues including human rights, for example, East Timor, Burma and the war in Chechnya. In 1999 he was also elected board member of the European Liberal Democrat and Reform Party. Since the end of 2001 he has been leader of the VVD Group in the European Parliament.

Before his election as an MEP Jules was Secretary General of the world union of liberal parties, the Liberal International, in London (1992-1999), during which time he was involved in supporting democratic movements in Asia, Latin America, Africa and Central and Eastern Europe. Prior to that (1986-1991) he was a municipal councillor in his hometown Amstelveen.

He began his political activities in 1979 as Personal Assistant to a Member of Parliament in the Netherlands (1979-1981), and went on to hold numerous other posts including Member and Chairman of the European Youth Policy group of the Dutch International Youth Council, and national Board Member of the Dutch Young Liberals. From 1985-1989 he was a member of the executive committee of Liberal International. In 1987 he co-authored a book on Dutch liberalism, and has published numerous articles on political issues.

Philippe Morillon MEP

Philippe Morillon graduated from St Cyr Military College in 1956, from SUPELEC - Ecole supérieure for studies relating to electricity in 1964 and the Army Staff College in 1974.

Philippe went on to become a General in the French Army, Commander of the United Nations Forces in Bosnia (1992-1993), and Commander of the Rapid Reaction Force (1994-1996).

He has been a Member of the European Parliament since 1999 and is currently the Chairman of the Fisheries Committee. He is also a member of the Foreign Affairs Committee, a member of the subcommittee on

Security and Defence and a member of the Euro-Mediterranean Parliamentary Assembly and of the ACP-EU Inter-Parliamentary Assembly. Philippe holds the distinction of Grand Officier of de la Légion d'honneur.

Bill Newton Dunn MEP

Bill Newton Dunn has been the Liberal Democrat MEP for the East Midlands since 2000. Previously he was a UK Conservative MEP for Lincolnshire from 1979 to 1994 and from 1999 to 2000.

He was educated at Gonville & Caius College, Cambridge, where he gained an MA degree in Natural Science, and afterwards at the INSEAD Business School, Fontainebleau, where he graduated with an MBA tri-lingual degree.

Bill stood as a UK Parliamentary candidate in both general elections in 1974. He then continued his career in industry until 1979 when he became a Conservative Member of the European Parliament. In 1993 he was elected Joint Leader & Chairman by the other 31 Conservative MEPs. Seeing that the Conservative Party had become increasingly negative about Britain's role in Europe, Bill crossed the floor to join the Liberal Democrats.

He is a member of the European Parliament's Committee on Citizens Freedoms (which covers Immigration, Asylum, Policing etc), also of the Committee on the Internal Market & Consumer Affairs, and a substitute member of the Committee on Budgetary Control. In March 2002 he became the Chairman of the UK Liberal Democrat MEPs, and is now their Whip.

Bill has written four books and several political pamphlets about Europe, the latest being 'Europe Needs an FBI.' He coined the phrase 'the democratic deficit' in a 1980s pamphlet.

Baroness Nicholson of Winterbourne MEP

Emma Nicholson was elected as a Member of the European Parliament for the South East region of England in June, 1999. She was re-elected as MEP for the same region in June 2004.

She currently serves in the European Parliament as Vice President of the Committee on Foreign Affairs, a Member of the Subcommittee on Human Rights, Substitute Member of the Committee on Culture and Education and Shadow Rapporteur for Romania. She is also a member of the Delegation for relations with Iran and the Euro-Mediterranean Parliamentary Assembly Delegation. She is responsible for gender mainstreaming issues for the Foreign Affairs Committee.

During the 5th Mandate of the European Parliament (1999-2004) she served as Vice President of the Committee on Foreign Affairs, Human Rights, Common Defence & Security Policy as well as Rapporteur for Iraq and for Romania, among other positions.

Baroness Nicholson was made a Life Peer in 1997 and takes the Liberal Democrat Whip. She served as a Member of the House of Commons from 1987 - 1997 and was Vice Chairman of the Conservative Party (1983 - 1987), joining the Liberal Democrats in 1995. Her NGO work includes the chairmanship of The AMAR International Charitable Foundation; Presidency of the Caine Prize for African Writing; Trusteeship of the Booker Prize for English Fiction and of the Booker Prize for Russian Fiction. She has also served as World Health Organisation Envoy for Health, Peace and Development since 2002.

Dr. Janusz Onyszkiewicz MEP

Janusz Onyszkiewicz is a Vice-President of the European Parliament. A former Polish Minister of National Defence (1992-1993, 1997-2000), and Deputy Minister for National Defence (1990-1992), Member of Polish Parliament (1989-2001), member of the Board of Center for International Relations (Warsaw), he was also press spokesman of the independent Solidarity trade union (1980-1989).

Janusz was awarded an honourary doctorate of the University of Leeds (1991). He has also been awarded with the Manfred Wörner Medal (Germany), the Order of the Grand Prince Gedymin of Lithuania, and the Grand Cross of the order of Leopold II (Belgium).

Bartek Nowak

A PhD candidate at the Warsaw School of Economics, Bartek Nowak has also taken Executive Studies at Harvard and the John F. Kennedy School of Government in Managing Political and Economic Reform (2005). He has an MA in Political Science (University of Silesia 2001). Currently in the European Parliament as the assistant of Vice-President Janusz Onyszkiewicz, he has been a Research Fellow at the Centre for International Relations in Warsaw (2003-2004), advisor to Polish Members of the European Convention on the Future of Europe (2002-2003). One of the leaders of the 'Yes' referendum campaign on Poland's entry to the EU, he also worked for the OSCE during the elections in Kosovo (2001).

Siiri Oviir MEP

After graduating from Tartu State University in 1974, Siiri Oviir went on to obtain a Masters in Law. She served as an assistant to the Chairman of the Supreme Court of the Soviet Socialist Republic of Estonia between 1975 and 1990.

She is a founder member of the Estonian Centre Party (Eesti Keskerakond) and has been a member of the Party executive since 1991. As well as having been a member of Tallinn City Council (1996-2002), Siiri was also an elected member of the Estonian Parliament during the

7th, 8th, 9th and 10th parliamentary terms (1992-2004) and the Deputy Speaker of the Estonian Parliament (1999-2001). Between 1990 and 1992 she was the Estonian Minister for Social Security and Minister for Social Affairs in 1995 and again 2002-3.

Siiri sits on the European Parliament Committees for Employment and Social Affairs, Women's Rights and Gender Equality as well as the Committee on Civil Liberties, Justice and Home Affairs. She is also a member of the Delegation to the EU-Armenia, EU-Azerbaijan and EU-Georgia Parliamentary Cooperation Committees and has been awarded the Badge of the Order of the National Coat of Arms, 5th class, the Medal of the Baltic Assembly and the Orthodoxer Konstantinscher Orden der Grossballi von Deutschland.

Karin Riis-Jørgensen MEP

Karin graduated in Law from the University of Copenhagen in 1978. From 1983 to 1986 she headed the international branch of the Danish Federation of Small and Medium-Sized Enterprises, based in Brussels. Then in 1987 she went to work for the European Commission's special branch for small and medium sized enterprises and in 1989 became head of department at international accountants Coopers & Lybrand (Price Waterhouse Coopers).

In 1994 Karin was returned for the first time as an MEP. Since 2004 she has held the position of Vice-Chair in the ALDE Group and in 2005 she became a board member of the think tank European Enterprise Institute.

She is a member of the European Parliament Committee on Economic and Monetary Affairs, and is a substitute member on the Committee on Internal Market and Consumer Protection. She is also a member of the Delegations for relations with China and the USA.

Anne E. Jensen MEP

Anne E. Jensen holds a master's degree in Political and Economic Science (Copenhagen University, 1978). She has previously worked as an Economist (1978-1984) at Privatbanken, and subsequently as the Chief Economist (1985-1994) at Privatbanken/Unibank. Between 1984 and 1985 Anne worked as a journalist and later became Senior Editor (1996-1998), Berlingske Tidende.

A director of the Danish Employers' Confederation (1994-1996), Anne was elected to the European Parliament for Venstre in 1999. She was Vice-Chairwoman of the Committee on Budgets (2002-2004).

Niels Busk MEP

Niels Busk was educated at Dalum Agricultural College. His past professional and political activities range from farming, reaching the rank of Major in Royal Life Guard Reserve (since 1981) to Chairman, Vice-Chairman and board member of various organisations and financial institutions (since 1981).

He has been a Member of the European Parliament since 1999 and a member of the Executive Board of the Danish Liberal Party, Venstre, since 1999.

He is currently a member of the Committee on Agriculture and Rural Development, a member of the Fisheries Committee, and a substitute member of the Environment, Public Health and Food Safety Committee.

István Szent-Iványi MEP

István Szent-Iványi graduated from university with a degree in Ethnography and Sociology in 1984. He went on to become a Member of the Hungarian national Parliament between 1990 and 2004, and in 1997-8 and 2000-02 was leader of his political Group.

Between 1994 and 1997 he was Secretary of State at the Ministry of Foreign Affairs and in 1998 through to 2002 chaired the Parliamentary Committee on Foreign Affairs. From 2002 to 2004 István chaired the Parliamentary Committee on European Integration.

His current responsibilities include sitting on the European Parliament's Foreign Affairs Committee and being a substitute member of the Committee on International Trade. He is also a substitute member of the Temporary Committee on Policy Challenges and Budgetary Means of the Enlarged Union 2007-13.

Graham Watson MEP

Graham Watson was elected to the European Parliament in 1994 after a 15 year career which spanned government, private sector and freelance professional positions.

In Parliament he has served on the Economic and Monetary Affairs Committee, the Budgets Committee and the Justice and Home Affairs Committee.

From 1999 - 2001 Graham was Chairman of the Justice & Home Affairs Committee. Among other things he secured Freedom of Information provisions allowing wide public access to EU documents, the passage of anti-terrorism and other crime fighting legislation. In January 2002 Graham was elected leader of the 53 strong group of Liberal Democrat and Reform MEPs. Today he leads the 105 MEPs of the Alliance of Liberals and Democrats for Europe Group.

Graham has written numerous articles for newspapers and magazines and has published five books about Liberal Democratic politics. Having lived and worked in Asia he is a frequent traveller to the Far East and is a regular commentator on Asia affairs. Graham is currently a Director of the Asia Pacific Public Affairs Forum.

Closer to home, Graham is the Chairman of the e-Parliament initiative, a project which promotes electronic exchange of information and opinions among legislators from around the world.

His hobbies and leisure interests include sailing and listening to jazz music. Graham lives with his wife and two young children (daughter born 1992 and son born 1995) in the small market town of Langport, Somerset.

Introduction

Globalisation is much talked about and widely analysed. Indeed, as my colleague Antonio Di Pietro points out, the internet search engine Google produces 65 million entries for globalisation, which is more than for climate change, famine or unemployment. Yet the set of phenomena we call globalisation has been relatively little studied through the prism of traditional political ideology. This collection of essays brings together thoughts about globalisation from 23 practising Liberal Democrat politicians from 12 different countries. As Members of the European Parliament, all have experience of working in a supranational political institution. These are their views on Liberal Democracy and Globalisation.

The reader will perhaps not be surprised at the amount of common ground between the contributors. They are, after all, all members of the same political group - the Alliance of Liberals and Democrats for Europe - in the European Parliament. A compendium with contributors from the left and right of the political spectrum would be a very different work. But the Liberal Democratic family is a broad church and one in which the differences of opinion between economic liberals and social liberals sometimes render agreement difficult, occasionally unreachable. What is significant in this collection of essays is that a common analysis of globalisation frequently leads the contributors to common conclusions. All believe that globalisation offers humankind greater opportunities than dangers, thus distinguishing Liberal Democrats from many members of the Social Democratic or Christian Democratic family. All see the development of the European Union as an essential tool for its member states in responding to globalisation and as a model for a wider approach to the supranational governance needed to cope with supranational challenges.

If some contributors stray a little from the topic of globalisation it is largely to concentrate on political challenges in France, where the referendum on the EU Constitution of May 2005 shook the political establishment. Yet since the issues at the top of French voters' minds were essentially related to the impact of developments in the outside world on a country which shares with Britain a peculiar insularity, such an approach is understandable.

Some contributors have followed my example of a wide ranging essay covering most if not all aspects of globalisation. Others have concentrated on particular causes and effects. Nonetheless I believe the result is a comprehensive statement of how Liberal Democrats in Europe perceive the global challenges we face.

Alfonso Andria MEP, like almost all other contributors, is optimistic about globalisation while recognising that some of its effects are not desirable. He argues that a global economy needs a solid foundation in shared values and institutional practices. The public perception of 'ungovernability' must lead politicians to develop new models of governance, he argues, from the local to the supranational, to cope with and to benefit from the phenomenon. He cites the American liberal philosopher John Rawls in defence of the need for greater political liberalism to combat market failure.

Emma Bonino MEP, like her UK colleague Sarah Ludford MEP, sees the greatest benefit of globalisation in the transfer of knowledge and information which enhance the protection of human rights. Drawing on her recent experience of working with women's rights groups in North Africa she describes women not only as the beneficiaries but also as the catalyst for democratic political reform in the region, seeing success in almost every Arab nation. International assistance is needed, she argues, 'using the language of freedom' since 'we cannot expect countries where democracy is challenged to bring about change on their own'. She claims that in the right environment globalisation can 'reduce inequality and smooth out economic discrimination and injustice' and that it has the potential 'to make the world a safer place'.

Jean-Marie Cavada MEP writes about the failure of Europe's political class to develop support for a united Europe and blames it on the lack of identifiable 'European public opinion'. He links this to the decline in public service broadcasting and suggests that this must be a priority area for EU policy.

Illustrating her essay with a fable about the sun and the wind, Maria Carlshamre MEP contrasts the approaches of the USA and EU to globalisation and concludes that the EU's 'soft power' approach is more likely to succeed in spreading the values of freedom and democracy around the globe. She sees the EU model of integration, based on respect for the rule of law, as being at the heart of Liberalism. Paradoxically, she says, the strongest opposition to the EU's power comes from within the EU itself. Nonetheless she believes that the American 'threat of interference' will never be as threatening as the EU's 'threat of non-interference'.

Marielle de Sarnez MEP, like her compatriot Jean-Marie Cavada, laments the failure of the recent referendum in France to produce a vote in support of the EU Constitution. She argues that France and the EU need each other and follows her analysis of the reasons for the 'No' vote with proposals about how France and the EU should move forward together. Excoriating the French political class for 'indolence or lack of courage', Marielle de Sarnez calls for greater honesty in political debate in her country.

A major challenge of globalisation according to Antonio Di Pietro MEP is to combat money laundering and associated financial crime. Lamenting the insufficiently developed legal tools available to the international community and the continued existence of tax havens, the Italian magistrate-turned-politician advocates the globalisation of rights and obligations and the criminalisation of money transfer for the purposes of tax evasion.

Slovenian MEP Mojca Drčar Murko draws lessons for today from the collapse of the liberal consensus in Europe in the first half of the twentieth century. She believes that globalisation of the economy is destroying the balance of the EU's social and economic policies and fears that Europe's middle class will not support the changes necessary in public policy to embrace globalisation. Drawing on the recent national elections in Germany and Poland she warns of the need to preserve the welfare state while conducting a stable monetary policy. Failure to do this will lead to the creation of a sub-class of citizens, she argues.

The virtues of Liberalism as a political ideology are extolled by Antoine Duquesne MEP (Belgium) in a strong defence of Liberalism's unique mix of freedom and responsibility. He sees the EU as a Liberal project which enhances Liberalism and serves as a source of aspiration beyond the EU, yet warns that the EU should not rest on its laurels in the face of new challenges. Liberalism needs no adjective, he argues, but must demonstrate 'active solidarity' to confound its critics.

Lena Ek MEP insists that economic liberalism in a global economy can produce the wealth required to fund social and environmental goals. Indeed, she sees environmental restitution as a priority. Like her Swedish colleague Maria Carlshamre, she believes the EU bears a responsibility for global development and must invest in knowledge and research to remain competitive. Unlike some other contributors, however, she is not totally dismissive of economic protectionism, believing that free trade can be good and bad and that some developing countries (such as India) can justify protection in some economic sectors.

Jelko Kacin MEP (Slovenia) looks at enlargement of the EU, particularly to the Western Balkans and to Turkey, as a phenomenon of and a response to globalisation. He insists that enlargement must only proceed on the basis of strict application of the Copenhagen criteria and that particular care is needed with Croatia and Serbia. A fervent advocate of Turkey's EU membership, Jelko Kacin argues that views in Western Europe are too often 'Eurocentric' and that the EU needs to look beyond its back yard to wider opportunities. This will involve jettisoning the 'dogma' surrounding the Common Agricultural Policy, he suggests.

Silvana Koch-Mehrin MEP (Germany) launches a strong defence of globalisation as a promoter of wealth, rights, higher wage and labour standards, environmental awareness and democracy. She believes it promotes democracy but poses, along with her counterpart Jules Maaten MEP of the Netherlands, the question of whether politicians are justified in embracing globalisation when those they represent often fear it. Looking at some of the world's major political entities, Koch-Mehrin believes that economic reform in China spurred by globalisation will lead to demands for democratic freedoms and suggests that Russia should have tried perestroika (economic reform) before glasnost (political liberalisation).

Sarah Ludford MEP states that in economic and social areas the balance sheet of globalisation is mixed, 'but the human rights account shows a healthy surplus'. The development of global civil society and the spread of information and knowledge about human rights has ushered in a 'values-led globalisation'. The individual enjoys opportunities for political influence through global NGOs which bypass national government and use 'the common language of respect and solidarity' to hold states to higher moral standards.

Posing the question 'who benefits from globalisation?', MEP Jules Maaten points out that globalisation and liberal democracy do not necessarily go hand in hand. Politicians must be able to demonstrate that globalisation brings greater opportunities than threats, he says. Claiming that international economic integration has allowed policy makers to deny some of their responsibilities in a way which is 'profoundly corrosive to democracy', the Netherlands MEP criticises the EU for its lack of a foreign policy and insists it must not leave the export of democracy to the USA.

Philippe Morillon MEP, who served as the head of UNPROFOR in Bosnia in the early 1990s, deplores the lack of altruism and international or intercommunal spirit in an increasingly interdependent world. Indeed, he detects a trend among human beings to exaggerate their differences, fuelling the fires of conflict. He studies too the French rejection of the EU's Constitution in the 2005 referendum and concludes that politicians must listen more to those they represent and that the EU should be tasked inter alia with preserving national identities.

Emma Nicholson MEP draws on her experience of work in the field of international adoption of children. She looks at the rapid growth of this practice and sketches how only now are national governments learning to control and regulate adoption to prevent abuse of children. She uses the example of Romania to show how such regulation can transform practices 'from among the worst to among the best in the world'.

International crime is the subject of a powerful essay by UK MEP Bill Newton Dunn, who outlines the scale of the phenomenon and castigates the lack of political leadership in tackling it effectively. Pointing out how short-term considerations and narrow political calculation are allowing criminal gangs to exploit the riches of the EU and the USA, causing untold misery, he calls for an effective cross-border approach to fighting crime.

Janusz Onyszkiewicz MEP examines the difficulties of making decisions globally without a global government. He looks at attempts to form such a government and concludes that a paradigm shift is required. Technical change will not be enough, he argues: institutions need to adapt and that requires political leadership. Nonetheless this Polish MEP (who is a Vice President of the European Parliament) is optimistic: the globalisation of democratic values and norms may be slow but it is inexorable.

Human freedom along the lines described by John Stuart Mill serves as the basis for Siiri Oviir MEP's analysis of the situation of women in countries emerging from the Soviet bloc. Drawing on her experience as Minister for Social Affairs in Estonia in the 1990s she argues that the situation of women got worse before it got better. Nonetheless, development towards EU norms of greater equality has been decisive and public attitudes are changing for the better.

Karen Riis-Jørgensen MEP, Anne E. Jensen MEP and Niels Busk MEP (all of Denmark) describe the current wave of globalisation as the second and one from which the EU is losing. They look particularly at economic globalisation and warn that the EU is falling badly behind the USA. They examine the reasons for this and outline what must be done to catch up.

István Szent-Iványi MEP also believes that the phenomenon of globalisation was much limited during the period 1917-89. He traces the first world's battle against the communist 'second' world and concludes that economic superiority, information flows and cultural domination were the main factors in the collapse of soviet communism. Similarly he believes that the phenomenon of globalisation will eventually bring down the other closed societies in the world and that Liberals and Democrats must exploit globalisation to spread freedom.

The major challenges drawn to our attention by our increasing global awareness are population growth, conflict prevention, education, environmental protection and fighting international crime according to Graham Watson MEP. Like István Szent-Iványi, I argue that Liberals must seize the opportunity of globalisation to meet these challenges and promote freedom and democracy across the world.

The British peer William Beveridge famously remarked that if you scratch the skin of a Conservative you will find a pessimist underneath. Scratch the skin of a Liberal, however, and you find an optimist. This book is a catalogue of optimism in the face of great challenges and not a little adversity. The contributors believe in humankind's innate capacity for good and ability to show solidarity. Indeed they seem to look forward with the French philosopher Victor Hugo to a day when the only battlefields will be those of markets open for business and the human spirit open for ideas. Or perhaps with the Irish poet Seamus Heaney to 'a time when hope and history rhyme'.

I hope you, the reader, will find reading these essays as stimulating as I do.

Graham Watson
Langport, Somerset
December 2005

Alfonso Andria MEP

Introduction

This is the world of globalisation - a new context for a new connectivity among economic and political actors throughout the world. Globalisation has been made possible by the progressive dismantling of barriers to trade and capital mobility, together with fundamental technological advances and steadily declining costs of transportation, communication and computing. Its integrative logic seems inexorable, its momentum irresistible. The benefits of globalisation are plain to see; faster economic growth, higher living standards, accelerated innovation and diffusion of technology and management skills; new economic opportunities for individuals and countries alike.

Why then, has globalisation begun to generate a backlash, of which the events surrounding the World Trade Organisation meeting in Seattle, November 1999, were the first but not the last visible manifestations?

A few people, groups or political forces oppose globalisation. They protest against its disparities. According to them, the benefits and opportunities of globalisation remain highly concentrated among a relatively small number of countries and are spread unevenly within them. In addition, they argue that in recent decades an imbalance has emerged between successful efforts to craft strong and well-enforced rules facilitating the expansion of global markets, while support for equally valid social objectives, be it labour standards, the environment, human rights or poverty reduction, has lagged behind.

Broadly speaking, for a number of people globalisation has come to mean greater vulnerability to unfamiliar and unpredictable forces that can result in economic instability and social dislocation, sometimes at lightning speed. There is also mounting anxiety in Europe that the integrity of cultures and national sovereignty may be at stake. Even in the richest EU countries people wonder who is in charge, fear for their jobs and worry that their voices are drowned out in the clamour of globalisation.

Globalisation - defined by Pope John Paul II as a "great sign of our times"[1] - is here to stay, there is no turning back. "We mustn't fool ourselves into thinking we can stop globalisation. This historical process must be tackled boldly and managed"[2]. Whether we like it or not, the world has become a global village. As previously mentioned, there are radically differing views about what constitutes globalisation. Many - but not all - in developed nations see it as the beneficial integration of markets, societies and nations. Many - but not all - in developing or emerging nations see it as the imposition of Western economic, social, cultural and political norms and standards. As always, *in medio stat virtus*[3].

Personally, I believe globalisation offers both a challenge and an opportunity. The only thing we can do is to grab the chances offered by globalisation by joining our forces to face the challenges, transforming them into opportunities[4]. We must extend the promise of globalisation to a much larger share of the population. We also need to engage in and elevate the global debate, to talk less about the problems we face - and who is to blame for them - and more about how we can, by working together, find solutions that benefit everyone. Friedman stated that "(Globalisation) can be incredibly empowering and incredibly coercive. It can democratise opportunity and democratise panic. It makes the whales bigger and the minnows stronger. It leaves you behind faster and faster, and it catches up to you faster and faster. While it is homogenising cultures, it is also enabling people to share their unique individuality further and wider"[5].

---

[1] Apostolic Letter *Novo Millennio Ineunte* of His Holiness Pope John Paul II to the Bishops, Clergy and lay faithful at the close of the great jubilee of the year 2000, 6 January 2001.

[2] Prodi, Romano. (2004) Semaines Sociales de France.

[3] Virtue stands in the middle.

[4] Rutelli, Francesco - Co-President of the EDP (European Democratic Party) and President of La Margherita-DL. Discorso al convegno nazionale delle Associazioni Cristiane Lavoratori Italiani (ACLI), Vallombrosa, 2001. (http://www.acli.it/rutelli.htm).

[5] Friedman, T., *The Lexus and the Olive Tree* (1999).

Globalisation and Governance

The economic geography of the world is changing. The economy is in part breaking its links with territorially and politically constituted entities and creating functional spaces of its own. These do not need to coincide with defined political entities.

Globalisation thus represents a major challenge to governance. In fact, globalisation fundamentally modifies the structural framework of world relations, as the role of the key actor which commonly defined both the international and the domestic relations - i.e. the State - is subject to a critical structural transformation.

From this perspective, the concept of globalisation itself seems inextricably linked to the idea of *ungovernability*. This association is understandable, since the classic focus of governance is the State, and the debate surrounding globalisation centres around the allegedly declining capacity of states to regulate what happens within their territories as a result of their increasing involvement in cross-border flows and networks[6].

In reality over the last two decades the traditional model of governance has increasingly failed to address peoples' needs. This scenario impels us to elaborate new models of 'governance' originating both at the supranational and at the local level. These must be capable of coping with the effects of globalisation while acquiring the best from it.

But globalisation also calls on us to develop a new political offer to meet the expectations of a wider polity.

Globalisation and the European Union

According to a traditional intergovernmental approach, global governance cannot receive direct democratic legitimisation, but must obtain its legitimacy indirectly through the participation of democratically elected governments in global policy making[7].

[6] Held, D. *Global Transformation: Politics, Economics and Culture (1999).*

[7] Grimm, D. 'Does Europe need a Constitution?', *European Law Journal*, Vol 1 No.3, November 1995 pp 282-302.

On the contrary, I consider that democratic legitimacy can and should be conferred through multiple channels in a pattern that corresponds to the pluralistic character of global governance. From this perspective, the European Union represents an exemplary model of supranational governance combining a traditional intergovernmental system with direct democratic legitimisation. The latter is assured through the European Parliament, the world's biggest multinational directly-elected institution.

The advent of monetary union among twelve EU Member States is a perfect example of that 'new governance' Europe is in need of. However, it has been the subject of extended debates. On one side there is the view that the new regime of European monetary governance and its 'stability culture' is nothing less than the imposition of a neo-liberal model of capitalism upon European states. Democratic authority over monetary policy is lost through 'Europeanisation' and the imperatives set are those of the most powerful interests in the global financial system. This directs governments to a position where welfare retrenchment is a notable and highly regrettable side effect of the Euro. However, it can also be argued that the pooling of monetary sovereignty is the most effective way for Europe to recapture the authority lost by governments to the forces of (financial) globalisation[8].

Hence, at a supranational level, the European Union - as the leading global market - has a key role to play. In the past fifty years it has shown that competition and mutual understanding are two essential complementary elements in order to strengthen and stabilise democracy and enhance economic welfare.

Therefore, the EU has to act as bridge and window between her Member States and the rest of the world, exporting her social and economic model in total respect of other cultures and traditions. The EU integration process and its international leadership must be encouraged.

---

[8] This is a crude polarisation of a complex issue. For more detail see Geoffrey R.D. Underhill 'Global Integration, EMU and Monetary Governance in the European Union: The Political Economy of the Stability Culture', in Kenneth Dyson (ed.) *European States and the Euro: Europeanisation, Variation and Convergence* (2002), pp. 31-52.

The Union has to push ahead the structural reforms in order to meet the ambitious Lisbon and Gothenburg agendas, take on more regional and global responsibilities and demonstrate that it can find effective solutions to the 'threats' of globalisation. "No European country, acting alone, can be a fully independent player in the globalised world. The strength to meet these challenges - the rise of the large Asian countries, the technology of North America or the migratory flows from the South of our planet - lies solely in the Union"[9].

Globalisation and the local dimension: 'Think Global, Act Local'

Both critics and enthusiasts of globalisation probably share a common powerful message: globalisation must mean more than bigger markets. Indeed, the economic sphere cannot be separated from the more complex fabric of social and political life, and sent shooting off on its own trajectory. To survive and thrive, a global economy must have a more solid foundation in shared values and institutional practices - it must advance broader, and more inclusive, social purposes and it must be compatible with local needs; it is, therefore, necessary to 'think globally and act locally'.

Borrowed from marketing campaigns, the exhortation to "Think Global, Act Local" has emerged as an organising focus for environmental politics. The *Agenda 21* process spawned a variety of local initiatives[10] and advocates of sustainable development emphasise the need for local participation in decision-making. This concept is intimately tied to the one of 'GLOCAL'[11], a digital neologism, which contains in itself the idea of co-existence of different territorial realities: the global and the local.

---

http://www.guardian.co.uk/Archive/Article/0,4273,4205514,00.html.
[9] Prodi, Romano. *Building our future together,* Speech to the European Parliament, (10th February, 2004).

[10] Lafferty, W. M. & Eckerberg, K., *From the Earth's Summit to Local Agenda 21 - Working towards Sustainable Development* (1998).

[11] On the concept of 'GLOCAL' see also De Rita, Giuseppe - Secretary General of CENSIS and former President of CNEL (Italian National Council for Economy and Labour - (1997) in *Manifesto per lo sviluppo locale, dall'azione di comunità ai Patti territoriali.*

Representation - democracy - could be described as an upstream and bottom-up process, reaching from villages and communities to local governments - the first of the layers that cover the globe completely - to other sub-national levels (states, cantons, provinces, prefectures, etc.) to sovereign states and various sub-regional coalitions of the willing (EU, G77, G8, etc.) to international and multilateral organisations, such as the UN or the international financing institutions.

However, in a world of equity and participation, representation is not a stable pyramid but a multi-dimensional dynamic process. All parts are linked to each other. 'Low' and 'high', 'up' and 'down' are not absolutes but contextual definitions. The local must be in direct dialogue with the global, as well as with the regional, national, and sub-sovereign.

On the basis of my former experience as a local administrator[12], I believe that only through local participation can the nature of political problems be properly identified and appropriate solutions to local social and environmental conditions found. Indeed, how could one realistically think of being global without first thinking local?

To meet the challenge for today's global governance, we need a synergy between vision and action and a well-balanced focus on both the global and local issues.

Empowering people at the local level emboldens them to take on issues beyond their immediate community. The phrase 'Think Globally, Act Locally' is, therefore, an 'instruction' to local politicians, associations and civil communities to promote an international agenda through which one can criticise the choices of governments or corporations.

Hence, the local dimension - which finds an important recognition in the EU's Constitutional Treaty - has an important role to play in the response to globalisation, as local authorities can develop policies to support local competitiveness in an increasingly dynamic and open economy. They also strive to make their industry competitive in the world economy, by offsetting the impact of delocalisation of business activity and

---

[12] President of the Province of Salerno from 1995 to 2004.

promoting the quality of life in their area. Thus, local authorities should respond to the challenges of globalisation by developing and pursuing integrated and coherent local development strategies, which should have long term view and a strong endogenous component, and the exchange of best practices between them should be further enhanced.

Sharing best practice involves the capture, dissemination and sharing of a work method, process, or initiative to improve organisational effectiveness, service delivery and citizen satisfaction. Local and regional authorities have a long history of defining needs, measuring performance, adapting and sharing best practices to ensure quality of service. This legacy of informally benchmarking a management practice, process or service, and then applying best practice is a foundation to build upon to promote a wider sharing of best practices. Applying formal benchmarks leads to the major improvements needed to meet present challenges.

In conclusion, there seems to be an invisible link connecting a tradition of good local governance and a high standard of living secured by a welfare state, equal opportunities among men and women, a high standard of education and health care, and a transparent society. If there really is an established link, those countries that have positive experiences in local self-government - constitutional and regulatory legal frameworks, decision-making processes, access to information, information technology systems, roles for the public domain, implementation of sustainability agendas, to list just a few examples - can regard this know-how as one of their most valuable export goods, one which they should be sharing with the rest of the world.

Globalisation and Liberal Democracy

However, new patterns of governance per se are not enough. They must be accompanied and driven by political vision. Politics cannot lag behind world changes, and this also rings true for political liberalism.

I see political democratic-liberalism as the never-ending attempt to rationalise the inner struggle between economic and social instances, which in a global contest obviously becomes more complex. From such a perspective, political democratic-liberalism is clearly not deaf to redistributive justice. It incorporates that too, but not as a goal, rather as an incumbent and utmost social obligation ethically rooted in the universal concept of human brotherhood.

True liberalism is never the Trojan horse for despotism, exploitation and unfair resource allocation. On the contrary, in a liberal democracy everyone must enjoy the same opportunities, regardless of social and geographical backgrounds. In Rawls' terms[13], each person is to have an equal right to the most extensive total system of equal basic liberties compatible with a similar system of liberty for all.

Conversely to the opinion of a few anti-global theorists, hence, it is quite unlikely that an unfair market may correspond to a liberal polity. On the contrary, market unfairness is often the predictable consequence of the lack of real freedom and competitiveness.

At present, developed countries rightly stand accused of hypocrisy: preaching free trade to the rest of the world, imposing trade liberalisation upon developing countries through the IMF and World Bank, but maintaining their own trade barriers to protect their own agriculture and other special interests. Protectionism is expensive, inefficient and ultimately ineffective, damaging taxpayers and consumers alike. However, as trade barriers fall, it becomes even more important to make sure that unfair competition is not re-established as a consequence of social dumping, commercial plagiarism and violation of intellectual property law.

Conclusions

We stand at historical crossroads. Nation states have come under greater pressure from globalisation. The nation state is not dead, but the rapidly changing world calls for both institutional and political innovation. A challenge that the European Liberals and Democrats are keen to take on board.

---

[13] Rawls, J. (1921-2002) American philosopher and Professor of Political Philosophy at Harvard University.

More effective implementation, transparency and a higher level of participation would be granted to citizens through greater involvement of local authorities in the policy-making process.

Local authorities play a crucial role in assessing the citizen's needs and offering immediate solutions to concrete issues, in a multi-dimensional dynamic process that puts them in direct contact with the supranational dimension.

The main task of supranational bodies should be to further enhance economic welfare and democratic reforms, through cohesive strategies and planning implemented on a subsidiarity level. In this scenario, the future course of the European Union is of crucial importance: the ratification process of the Constitutional Treaty, the further enlargement and integration of current Member States, the structural market reforms and the implementation of the Lisbon and Gothenburg agendas. In the age of globalisation, this project is our real capital and we must do our best to maximise its yield.

Emma Bonino MEP

Globalisation comes in many guises and takes many forms. The traditional view says that through developments in technology the world has become smaller, creating one global marketplace. Capital, goods and labour markets - and particularly capital markets - have all become increasingly globalised. This perspective explains globalisation as the unimpeded flow of goods and people and the opening up of new markets.

But this is only one viewpoint, one interpretation. Globalisation is a subject that will increasingly shape the lives of nations and individuals. It is a deeply emotive issue with significant political ramifications. It can be understood in more ways than simply through an economic lens - the Ricardo or Adam Smith 'wealth of nations' view - that the economic pie gets bigger if countries trade with one another. On the ground, the exposure of countries to a global market is having profound effects on other aspects of life, specifically the spread of democracy and the consequential beneficial impact that it has on human rights.

An abstract view of the process of 'political globalisation' is not enough. Real political action and reform are spreading from nation to nation, in the footsteps of economic globalisation: as one nation discovers the benefits of trade and transparency, its neighbours look on closely.

Economic and political globalisation are two sides of the same coin. Political reform is a function and also partly a consequence of capital flows and investment. Basically, capital is most likely to be attracted to and stay in a politically stable environment and less likely to go to unstable areas. It is no coincidence that direct foreign investment in Russia has declined following a government crackdown on business and - more importantly - media freedom.

Across the world capital flows and trade are opening the door to reform in political institutions and the expansion of human rights. There must be political stability for a nation to become the recipient of economic globalisation. This is exactly the carrot and stick approach that resulted in writing off national debt for some African nations: get your house in order and you will benefit economically.

The first tentative green shoots of democratic reform can now be seen growing across the Middle East. With elections this year in the Palestinian territories, Iraq and soon in Egypt, democracy is on the rise. This is accompanied by the democratisation of gender, and in countries such as Bahrain and Qatar the implementation of women's suffrage. Women are benefiting from political globalisation in a way they have not previously under old-style political and social systems. They are finally being able to speak with a voice that had been muffled for too many generations. The emergence of women's rights, coupled with a political voice, is one of the most significant aspects of the process of political globalisation.

While political actors, scholars and NGOs all agree that increased reform and democratisation will help improve the status of women in the region, they miss the vital point: that women can potentially trigger the drive forward to democracy in the Arab world. We must recognise that they are active motors for change. Emerging rights for women have the potential to be the fuel powering the spread of democracy across the region.

I believe that political reform is critical for two key reasons. Firstly, democracy is essential for development. If women are active in political life they can unleash 50% of the development potential of countries where women are currently unheard and under-represented. Nations that continue to exclude women from the economic mainstream will never exploit their full potential and will forego the economic benefits that flow from women as generators of economic growth. Secondly, women have much to offer to the political debate. Political discourse is weaker in societies where women are silent citizens. In just one generation in Europe, we have seen the benefits of women gaining full rights in society. Remember it was only in the 1970s when in France women were first able to open their own bank accounts; in Switzerland women were first given the vote; and in Italy divorce was introduced.

Because women are fighting for their individual rights in societies where collective rights are traditionally of great importance, these events are tantamount to a cultural revolution. This is the Middle East's hidden democratic revolution. Women are fighting for change across many areas. Personal issues such as divorce, custody of children and economic rights are now on the agenda, as are campaigns against the horrific practice of 'honour killings' and female genital mutilation.

Evidence of the winning of basic political rights is not hard to find. There are successes in almost every Arab nation. For example, in Saudi Arabia, women are close to securing the right to vote. Some have already declared their readiness to stand as political candidates in municipal elections, a major achievement given that just two years ago, the mere idea of women voting was rejected on the basis of cultural religion. Women in the Palestinian territories have started their own democratic journey too. Two thirds of the electorate voted in the Gaza and West Bank Presidential election. Half of these were women.

In Yemen and Egypt there are moves to include women in the political process through a form of affirmative action or quotas. Quotas I believe are not the solution; women cannot achieve fair representation through a game of mathematics, but I do recognize that this is an important step. In Algeria, Morocco and Egypt, laws have been introduced, providing basic rights for women when it comes to family law. The wife of a high profile Egyptian actor recently won the right to use a DNA test to prove her ex-husband fathered her son, something that would have been unthinkable not too long ago.

Kuwait is leading the movement in securing political and democratic rights for women. The appointment of the country's first ever female minister is a major milestone and two years from now women will take part in parliamentary elections for the first time. Alongside this the government has appointed two women as members of its municipal council, the first women to be appointed to the body. Just a few years ago these achievements would have been inconceivable, but the political landscape has shifted quickly and dramatically. I hope that this victory will pressure neighbours like Saudi Arabia to accept that women must be free to use their political voice.

These are very encouraging signs and even Saudi Arabia has its own success story: it has been announced that women in Saudi Arabia will be able to apply for driving licences for the first time, something they were previously barred from doing. These slow but incremental steps together create the movement that will drive change across the Middle East.

Whilst these developments are promising, we must accept that some of the issues facing women cannot be solved solely through a legislative process. In Jordan and Syria the practice of 'honour killings' continues. The representation of women in politics will not bring an immediate end to this practice; it will, however, slowly demonstrate that women have rights equal to men. That change in perception I hope will be the catalyst for undoing a practice that cannot be tolerated in or by any country in the world. The same is true for female genital mutilation, but at least in that case there are some signs that attitudes are changing and that awareness is driving change.

Women have an important and central role in effecting democratic change. We all have a responsibility to help the advancement of women across the world. Where women are being denied their rights - be it voting, education or personal equality - we must act collectively. The better-established democracies must do everything in their power to support these developments in order to coax and encourage the process that is already underway.

Momentum is key in encouraging the positive changes and disabling the negative. All nations must offer support to these causes, led by Europe and the United States. The international community cannot just be an onlooker, offering encouraging but empty words; instead it must play a crucial part by providing advice, resources and - fundamentally - ways of integrating and linking these different campaigns, providing a forum for ideas. We must use the language of freedom. It is the notion of freedom that has and will spur people on to call for change and through freedom, comes stability.

A recent initiative by the US State Department to help create a women's network in the region so that women can share and learn from each other is a very positive move. We need to connect ourselves with them because with our support they become more courageous and vocal. The intention of the EU to extend the Barcelona process to the Middle East, building a strategic partnership across the region will also benefit this process.

We cannot be distracted in our efforts. We are at a critical juncture where momentum could just as easily ebb away as expand and move forward. Too many people still live under oppressive and cruel regimes, with little hope of effecting much real change. The bloody suppression of protestors in the Uzbek city of Andijan clearly demonstrated that we cannot expect change to occur on its own. Countries such as the United States and European nations must take the lead and create the environment for economic reform or face a drift towards extremism as the result of a potent mix of radicalism and poverty.

Against this backdrop, we must therefore continue international efforts to strengthen worldwide initiatives in favour of democracy not just for the benefit of women but for the benefit of all, and across all continents. Specifically this means groups such as the Community of Democracies taking a much more proactive and visible role. I believe that to foster and promote democracy a 'democratic coalition', with its capacity for undertaking collective actions on major issues in international politics, is a critical and important first step. This group would be different from the United Nations, where every country regardless of its attitude to human rights, particularly to political rights, has a place at the table. But there must be strict and unequivocal criteria for membership.

In the same way that human rights and democratic values are tacitly considered a 'must' for European Union membership, these same values, which are also reflected in the UN Charter and the Universal Declaration of Human Rights, must be the centrepiece of membership of the 'democratic coalition'. The timely proposal for the creation of a more robust Council of Human Rights equipped with a 'Democracy Fund' for the purpose of assisting emerging democracies should help in this endeavour.

It is becoming more and more imperative to reinforce the value of co-ordinated initiatives across continents in sharing common democratic values of freedom, the rule of law, and the protection of human rights. This can help build common positions and proposals in the international arena, including within the United Nations, and can act as a catalyst to attract new countries to the ever-increasing group of democracies. We cannot expect countries where democracy is challenged to bring about change on their own. There must be something to strive for - a sense of belonging to a wider community of values - and with it a change in economic conditions and opportunities.

In the right environment, globalisation can reduce inequality and smooth out economic discrimination and injustice. It has the potential to make the world a safer place, breaking down borders, confronting and overcoming intolerance and giving people a voice in their political future. I believe that this era of economic, social and technological globalisation would not make much sense unless we all share and experience the essential universal values of democracy and human rights. It is in everybody's common interest to support the current openings and movement towards reform. We must not miss this opportunity because there is too much at stake. To secure stability in the world everyone must be able to express their own political will and be free to determine their own lives. I am certain that in the era of globalisation, the prize we must all strive for is democracy and rights for all.

Maria Carlshamre MEP

"If you don't do as the US wants, you will be punished. If you do as the EU wants, you will be rewarded."

The challenge was truly global. The Wind turned to the Sun, saying with confidence, "I am stronger than you".

Whereupon the Sun replied, "Maybe, but I am not willing to take your word for it. Let us take a challenge."

"A challenge?"

"Yes. Do you see that man down there on the road?"

"Yes, what about him?"

"Let's see who can get his clothes off first, you or me."

"Easy!" said the Wind.

A gale soon blew up. The man walking along the road had difficulties with every step, but tried as hard as he could to move forward, holding tightly onto his hat and coat.

The gale grew and turned into a storm. The man fell to his knees. But he held on to his clothes as if his life depended on it.

"Can I have a go?" the Sun asked softly.

The clouds began to disappear and the storm calmed down.

The man picked himself up and started walking again. The sky turned from grey to blue and the sun kept shining. At first the warmth was wonderful, but after a while the man began to sweat. He walked on, but with the temperature rising he decided to take his coat off, followed by his hat. But even in his shirtsleeves, he was still very hot. Arriving at a small lake, he gave in, took the rest of his clothes off and jumped into the water.

Independence from external intervention, having full control over a certain territory has always been the core element of statehood. But through the European Union the different peoples of Europe have turned this old definition upside down. Instead of guarding our sovereignty from external interference, we have turned mutual interference and surveillance into the basis of our security.

Over the last few decades European Union law has become national law through a large number of common standards and regulations -

approximately half of all national legislation is now in fact EU legislation. In practice this means that the power of the EU is invisible. This might create the impression that the EU is somehow sneaking in while our backs are turned. Maybe this feeling of insecurity is one of the reasons why many citizens feel so negatively towards the EU.

Apart from citizens' discontent with the way the EU is working, this principle of mutual interference and surveillance has also had deep effects on how we deal with countries outside the Union. A lot of energy has recently been devoted to the internal discord of the European Union - the referenda on the Constitution in France and the Netherlands, the continuing divisions among the Member States, the weakness of the common will, the lack of popular support, the democratic deficit - there are indeed numerous reasons to watch present developments with pessimism. On top of this, we are still in the process of understanding the implications of the recent enlargement to 25 Member States when it comes to the internal structure of the Union.

Europe grew from 6 to 15 and became more effective in the process, but the recent referenda may be seen as an indication of growing discontent in the old Member States towards the new. Europe is no longer an exclusive club for a limited number of well-to-do Western European countries.

Another issue high on the agenda is what to make of the war in Iraq. From London, Paris and Berlin to Stockholm and Copenhagen, the European reactions to US foreign policy were divided, to put it mildly. From some quarters it was concluded that these divisions were a sign of weakness and that our Union would continue to be politically irrelevant for as long as we cannot manage to speak unanimously. But in a recent book, *Why Europe will run the 21st century¹*, Mark Leonard makes an excellent case for the opposite interpretation - that although Europe doesn't have one leader, a network of different centres of powers could instead turn out to be a strength, rather than a weakness. The provocative title of Leonard's book is not to be taken literally. In a recent article in

---

¹ Leonard, M., *Why Europe will run the 21st century* (2005).

Prospect magazine[2] he underlines the basic idea behind his suggestion that we are about to witness the emergence of a new European century. He concludes "Europe will not run the world as an empire, but the European way of doing things will have become the world's". In the midst of pessimism and crisis, it is time we started talking not only of the failures of the Union but of its successes.

What then is, according to Leonard, the most important success of 'the European way of doing things'? Precisely this: it is giving birth to a new concept of power, where national security is based on mutual interference and surveillance instead of the old idea of independence from external intervention. It is often said that the European Union is difficult to understand. There is at least one simple reason for this: it does not fit into our established categories. It is not a state; neither is it a federation nor a confederation. Mark Leonard describes it as "a network rather than a state" and points out that this network redefines power as surveillance. This new kind of surveillance makes the old concept of statehood obsolete. No wonder there is confusion and division - we are in uncharted territory.

One way to examine this completely new kind of power is to compare it to the strongest exponent of the old system in today's world: the United States of America. There is no doubt that the US is the world's only remaining superpower. In military terms no other country comes even close to having the same strength. At the same time it is equally obvious that the more this empire tries to get its way, the less it succeeds in reaching its global goals. The war on terror has created an unparalleled upsurge in anti-Americanism. And in the shadow of this war, newly emerging international patterns are visible, notably the ever-growing presence of China.

In the traditional system of independent states each and every country tries to get its will done. Through negotiations, discussions, trading - and as the last resort - violence. A state relies ultimately on the threat of intervention to secure its interests. The logic of this system is sovereignty and national security, at its worst, national isolation and

---

[2] Leonard, M., 'Ascent of Europe' *Prospect* No.108, March 2005.

protectionism, with the use of force towards any kind of intrusion. It is a system that favours states with military power. From the point of view of the traditional system of states the EU is weak. The power of Europe is not measurable in military budgets. In one respect the power of the EU is also difficult to see. Maybe this is one of the reasons it is so difficult to grasp what the Union is all about. Not democratic deficit *per se*, but rather a lack of basic visibility. This anonymity is built into the very structure of the EU.

More than half of all legislation stems from Union law, working through the existing political structures at Member State level. The influence of the EU becomes invisible, more a matter of substance rather than form. But apart from the internal discord with this lack of visibility, it has also made the power of the EU less provocative to the outside world. Somewhat paradoxically, the strongest opposition to this power is inside the Union, not outside.

In the 1990s the EU failed miserably in the wars surrounding the breakdown of former Yugoslavia. In the end, the military force of the US and NATO was necessary to put an end to this ongoing outrage in the back yard of our continent. Why the EU failed so completely here remains to be thoroughly analysed. One reason is discernible in the aftermath of the Iraq war; the strength of the US is its military power whilst the strength of the EU is building peace. Following the Balkan wars, the EU has found a way to deal with unrest and human rights abuses in our neighbourhood. The success story of the Ukraine to date is a good example of this. We can now start to see the basic difference between the European and American ways.

While the American 'power' was typified at the time of the birth of the nation state, the European 'power' is still in the making, as a consequence of the dismantling of the nation state in our part of the world. The nation state as a form of political organisation was born in our part of the world about 500 years ago. By the beginning of the 20th century the last remnants of the old ways of political organisation, i.e. feudal states, city states and empires, had disappeared on our continent. And by the second half of the 20th century Europeans were ready to move on.

The US, in the beginning a mere satellite to the old kingdoms of Europe, developed in its own way. Many Americans today see their country as somehow above nationalism. Patriotism is a stereotypically American word, often seen as something other and better than the fading and destructive concept of nationalism so common in Europe. This has created a basis for the American way of seeing their country as an exception. Sometimes this feeling of exception has fostered a deep sense of isolationism; other times it has paved the way for a missionary zeal towards the rest of the world.

But even though the US was born out of the Enlightenment ideas of universal values, it was nevertheless formed in practice out of the experiences of 19th century rapid nation state building. And today it is obvious that in matters of international relations the US is one state among others, albeit the strongest one. In today's world the US is the strongest among equals - even if the Americans do see themselves as an exception. The EU on the other hand, represents a new phase, leaving the old system of nation states behind. And the difference between the US and the EU has far-reaching consequences, particularly concerning the ways in which Europe and America have dealt with their respective neighbours in recent years. We face similar threats - trafficking in drugs, weapons and human beings, large flows of illegal migrants, internationally-organised crime, but the way in which these issues are confronted are profoundly different.

"Send in the Marines!" is the battle cry symbolising the core of US foreign policy. In the last half century the US has sent troops into neighbouring countries more than 15 times, but these countries, including Granada, Colombia, Haiti, Guatemala and indeed Cuba, have barely changed. Moreover, the US has in many cases been forced or felt forced to re-deploy troops to these areas. While the US threatens invasion as a last straw when another country doesn't obey, European power is based on the opposite tactic of non-interference - not the threat of intervention, but the opposite threat of not intervening - of withdrawing the prospect of membership.

With the possible exception of Belarus, there is nothing worse for countries such as Turkey, Serbia, Croatia, Ukraine, Bosnia and Moldova than for Brussels to stop interfering in their internal affairs. Closing the doors completely means closing the doors to possible future membership. Even in the case of Turkey, where it has been explicitly stated that it will take years, if not decades for Turkey to become a Member State, this hope remains a forceful instrument for change towards democracy and greater respect for human rights.

This new kind of power is exemplified by the future decisions anticipated to be taken by Turkey abolishing capital punishment and ending the criminalisation of adultery. One consequence of this indirect, almost invisible power is that it is not perceived as a challenge to the rest of the world. Nowhere in the world are the flags of the EU being burnt, and nowhere are the institutions of Europe targets for hostility, in the way the star spangled banner and American institutions are. So far there is no sign that other countries want to curb our influence. This is especially true of our closest neighbours. The European Union is a giant in our part of the world, but instead of fearing it, adjacent countries want to join.

The European power is based on the idea of making others adhere to fundamental norms rather than getting our way on each decision. Because of this it is crucial how we ourselves handle issues of fundamental rights inside our Union. What we demand of others we have to abide by ourselves. Otherwise a clear signal will be sent to the outside world and what we will get is mere lip service and no real commitment. This places a heavy burden on the European commitment to basic principles of democracy and fundamental rights. Respect for these values cannot be seen as icing on the cake of economic growth and prosperity. There is a fundamental reason why complete dedication to the rule of law in every circumstance is necessary, including when the call for a war on terrorism is all the rage. Without this commitment, the whole foundation of our Union would crumble.

This commitment is, and has been since the beginning of liberal ideas, the core of Liberalism. Might is not right, but the rule of law certainly is. And the basic liberal combination of economic prosperity and respect for civil liberties is still a model waiting to be implemented in many parts of the world. The power of the EU can therefore be seen as a typically liberal kind of power and as a model for the future. Mark Leonard describes a possible future where the world "will not be centred around the US or the UN, but will be a community of interdependent regional clubs" based on the EU principle of interfering in each other's affairs, and promoting peace and the rule of law. Even though there are several reasons to watch the present development in Europe with pessimism, let us therefore not forget how far we have come and the great opportunities ahead.

The basic difference between the EU and the US could ultimately be described as the difference between punishment and reward. If you fail to do as the US wants, you will be punished. However, if you do as the EU wants, you will be rewarded. Therefore, the Sun's words to the Wind on her victory could also be the words of Europe towards America, "Your strength just created an opposition that in the end became impossible to overcome. My warmth gave him a reason to do as I wanted, because he wanted to himself. That is true strength!"

Jean-Marie Cavada MEP

Is there such a thing as European public opinion? Very rarely! But when it does exist, it is passionate, hard-hitting and incisive, and it upsets our rather introverted institutions with their tendency to just muddle along. There was something surreal about seeing the European Council in despair after meeting in June 2005; about watching the European Commission, inevitably rocked by the crisis, shamed by its passivity, but continuing nevertheless to churn out its legislative work as if nothing was happening and about seeing Parliament sitting in its committees and plenary sessions as if the construction of Europe were not threatened. On the other side of this façade lay the most indescribable chaos: over ten countries have ratified or will ratify the Constitutional Treaty but two have refused in a kind of fierce retribution, for here is the latest illustration of the existence of European opinion, or rather nationalistic opinions, on the European idea. The rather moving offer of the ten new entrants from Central and Eastern Europe to tighten their financial belts to serve the egoism of the big nations is a good lesson here in European politics, or rather faith in the Union, despite what ulterior motives may have existed.

I am often asked whether the media in Europe bears some responsibility for this loss of faith, amid this cacophony and in the face of so little courage from certain groups of leaders. My reply is yes, of course. But in order to learn positive lessons from this hard fall, we need to examine the relationship between national and European institutions and the overwhelming lack of embodiment of what is happening in Brussels in the eyes of the people. The first place on the roll of honour for good media coverage of European news must go to the written press. Not a day goes by without descriptions or analyses of EU decisions appearing in the major daily papers of the 25 Member States. There is something bizarre in their approach to the EU, which avoids mention of the work of the European Parliament despite the fact that it is more powerful than many national parliaments. This approach favours coverage of the EU's executive work. In second place is broadcast news and mainstream radio stations. Europe exists here, but only to a certain extent. Representation of the work of the European institutions on the radio is often filtered through the prism of the host nation, as is the case with television. It's also a shame that decisions taken on issues genuinely affecting the lives of European citizens are given less coverage than the obsequiousness of the institutions, power struggles and occasional scandals. But enough said!

There is a far wider gap when it comes to the reporting of national television stations within the 25 Member States on decisions taken in Brussels. Although my professional past compels me to be discreet about this, my present role in public life obliges me to speak plainly. So I will do this by analysing the system as a whole rather than by listing its good and bad points.

The history of television in post-war Europe tells the story of a gradual move away from state monopolies towards a landscape that includes a host of private television stations, not all of which feel obliged to acknowledge the strict duty to provide information to the same degree. We will ignore the pure entertainment stations that give little room to news coverage - this is a strategic choice that accompanies their market positioning. But the remainder, which in Europe account for between 65% and 85% of the market depending on the country, provide an interesting picture. They take one of two attitudes. Some include European news in their main news programmes on an almost daily basis, although there is insufficient comparison of lifestyles, initiatives, capacity for reform or social, economic and financial problems. But Europe does exist for them. It is a pity that in countries where at least 60% of national legislation consists primarily of transposed European directives, European issues are not given as much coverage as domestic issues. But we must recognise that although about half a dozen countries have a sizeable section devoted to the EU, occasionally as part of specialist programmes, these are often unfortunately at off-peak viewing times. Meanwhile television channels in the second category do little to keep their viewers informed and have no policy of covering major decisions taken within the European institutions.

More interesting still is the consideration the European Commission and Parliament will have to give to the future organisation of television.

Until now there has been only one directive on television without frontiers. It was mostly concerned with the means of transmission rather than the content. Over the past few years conflicts and evolutions have mostly been regulated purely by competition and by free market operation. But the letter and the spirit of our rules force us to look at the future in terms of two central questions. Firstly, do we want a reasonable balance between public and private services? Or do we think public broadcasting will become merely a remnant of the past that we don't dare to destroy (i.e. sell off privately) but that shrinking budgets will end up slowly strangling? Secondly, does the supplementary commercial income that managers of public television budgets must increasingly depend upon influence information content, particularly with regard to its place and frequency in the programming schedule and the time of broadcasting? It doesn't take a Marxist to see the link between programming choices and the need to take the biggest share of the audience at peak viewing times and hence to gain the greatest commercial revenue. Indeed, it is common knowledge that it is through advertising revenue that public broadcasting directors gain margin for manoeuvre, where this is allowed. It should ring alarm bells that three quarters of public television broadcasters in the 25 Member States are experiencing serious financial difficulties. If they are not, this is due to government-imposed constraints on their future development in new media. This has the effect of preventing them from contributing new content in a competitive market against private companies, for which they are increasingly failing to provide modern competition.

In the Committee on Civil Liberties, which I chair, I've noticed that one thing we need to be constantly vigilant about in the Charter of Fundamental Rights is pluralism. There is a link between vitality of pluralism and the economic diversity of public and private television broadcasters. The Member States and European institutions do not naturally feel the need to get involved with the content of programming schedules. There are management teams as part of the channel leadership to do that. However, they are accountable to citizens for the fact that governments are only encouraging one sort of competition, from the bottom: competition between the private channels. Although this is needed, it is not enough. Genuine pluralism is about being able to choose regularly between entertainment programmes, cultural programmes, music and sport, but also reporting and discussion of the life that affects their future as European citizens. The fact that in the United Kingdom, where the Broadcasting Act pioneered within Europe aims to balance the public and private sectors, the BBC has undertaken three sets of redundancies and is questioning the validity of the sale of one of its global networks, means something has gone wrong. In Germany, which for a long time set the standard to my mind on the notion of balance, I was shocked this year to see for the first time the recommendations of the KEF (the body responsible for determining the financial requirements of broadcasting institutions) being rejected by some *Länder,* which reduced the budgets recommended by this independent federal commission, unchallenged until now. In Central and Eastern Europe, public radio and television broadcasters have not yet extracted themselves from the grip of the governments to which Communist tyrannies enslaved them. Words fail me regarding the sinister mess of television broadcasting in Italy. Management teams need to think in audiovisual terms rather than in terms of cynical wheeling and dealing and contempt for democracy. Exceptions include hopes for a Spanish revival (although there is much to do) and the fragile and temporary status quo in France.

We cannot claim to open up the debate on life in Europe without daring to challenge entrenched opinions: it is the role of governments, but it is now also the role of the European Union to get involved in firmly introducing a better balance into broadcasting services, which must mean a better economic balance between public and private services. But let's not forget the sudden arrival of a new European voice on the Internet and through mobile phones. These are media that are unregulated sometimes to the point of indecency, immorality or irresponsibility. But generally they offer a wonderful way for the oppressed to make themselves heard by the world. In our Europe, if only during the Spanish general elections in March 2004, they provided a forum within twenty-four hours for challenging the word of the incumbent government, which was determined only to see the hand of the Basque separatist movement in the Madrid bomb attacks, even though the special forces themselves were casting doubt on this version of the facts. Mr Aznar's conservatives were swept away by widespread text messaging. If further proof were required of our need to watch over the balance of the economic systems that govern the media, the role that European citizens should occupy within them and the analysis and criticism of the decisions of its institutions, it is here.

Whatever we do not readily debate in the public arena will fortunately break into it anyway.

Marielle de Sarnez MEP

There is something uncanny about the total silence regarding Europe which has reigned since the referendum on the Constitution. The dismayed or embarrassed silence of all political leaders has been matched by the silence of the governments as if unable to face up to the reasons for the 'no' vote or to offer any fresh prospects for Europe. We must break the silence today so as to rebuild tomorrow.

The outcome of the vote of 29th May was more than just the aftershock of 21st April 2002[1] and is symptomatic of an extremely deep-seated crisis fuelled by questions over French identity. This is reflected in the feelings of anxiety experienced by our fellow citizens in an increasingly open and global world with no familiar landmarks. This social, economic, political and moral crisis has sent shock waves throughout Europe. The temptation to withdraw behind national borders, the victory of national chauvinism and intolerance, the ground lost by political Europe, the doubts expressed concerning the euro, the criticisms levelled at the Common Agricultural Policy, and total failure to reach agreement on the European Union budget all show that Europe is not only encountering difficulties but, far more seriously, is losing momentum and sliding back into the most serious crisis it has ever faced.

A correct diagnosis of the reasons for the 'no' vote is thus all the more necessary. A non-existent, mistaken or purely notional diagnosis could prove fatal to the project in which we have been engaged for 50 years, while a correct one will set the horizon not only for Europe but also for France. It is striking to note how the crisis in France is linked to the crisis in Europe. Europe cannot be built without France, nor France without Europe.

The 'no' vote showed us a France split into two, a divided country in which 4 million are unemployed or receiving the basic minimum income, where almost a quarter of young people are unable to find work,

---

[1] Jean-Marie Le Pen of the *Front National* got through to the second round of the French Presidential Elections.

where it is by no means unusual for a pensioner who has worked his entire life to have only 50 euros a week left to live on once he has paid his rent, where 3 million live in sub-standard accommodation and where even the middle classes find it hard to make ends meet as a result of frozen salaries and rising prices.

The vote on 29th May was therefore very much divided along the lines of class, those voting 'yes' being in the company director (55%), professional (60%), or executive (67%) bracket and those voting 'no' being clerical staff (63%), manual workers (70%) and the unemployed (76%). The 'no' voters were those French citizens who had been promised much by the elite but ultimately received little, and who obviously did not believe that their problems could be solved in 100 days. The most dangerous thing of all would be to underestimate their anxieties.

In addition to issues affecting France, there are those issues relating to Europe. As in 1992, the referendum aroused passionate debate, the likes of which had not been seen for a very long time, dividing parents and their children, colleagues and friends. And here an initial paradox is emerging: while our nation is passionate about Europe as an issue, in 15 years it has been given only two opportunities to give its views. Everything it has ever wanted to say about Europe has, on two occasions, crystallised around referendum issues. In 1992 the issues at stake were the euro and the popular debate on Europe and individual nations, while in 2005 they concerned the Constitution and the public debate regarding the social model and enlargement.

It is now time to make politicians more aware of their responsibilities. Popular misconceptions regarding the functioning of Europe, its institutions and its history contrast starkly with the role played by France from the outset. For years, our national leaders have, through indolence or want of courage, chosen to make Europe the scapegoat for all our problems, all too often holding it up to ridicule where they should have been holding it up as a symbol, as something of immediate value. Furthermore, the question of enlargement was a source of concern and anxiety for many of our citizens, since our leaders failed to explain it properly, if at all. It is enough to look at what was done or rather not done in France to mark this historic date in the process of reunification of our continent. There were no celebrations or solemn declarations and no events were organised. While 1st May was a day of jubilant celebration in Eastern Europe, in France it passed by in silence! Each time the people are ignored and decisions concerning them taken in secret they will show their disapproval of those who govern them in this manner.

There is a historical reason for this gulf between Europe and its citizens. Europe is first and foremost the union forged after three lethal wars between France and Germany. At the time of Schuman and Monnet, the people were not ready for reconciliation and the construction of Europe. Thus it was, from the outset, that political, economic and cultural leaders set their course with no regard for the people, who have now chosen to return the compliment. After 29th May, one thing is certain: if we do not build Europe together, Europe will not exist. It is only when the people of Europe are actually involved in its construction that it will be able to take shape and achieve its own identity.

Europe's identity is in fact the crux of the matter, as revealed by the question of Turkish accession. We have said from the outset that the issue at stake is not Turkey itself but the nature and identity of Europe. European leaders having refused to provide an answer, the French voters have vented their exasperation.

We are now calling on our leaders to return to the task in hand since we are not willing to resign ourselves to the imminent demise of a political Europe. Everything we said during the campaign about the need for Europe, a strong Europe for ourselves and for the world, is truer now than ever before.

We need a programme and a calendar of work and, as MEPs, we have a particular role to play. Even if it were legally possible, it would not appear to be politically viable to hold a second vote in France on the same draft Constitution. Once the ratification process has been completed, we must therefore proceed to rework the draft, concentrating on the first part relating to the objectives of the Union and its institutions. There is no need to review the Charter of Fundamental Rights since it was widely approved. As for the third part, which is merely a compilation of existing treaties, I do not believe that it really belongs in the Constitution.

What will be the time scale? Deliberations on the text will last for several months. The European elections in 2009 would be a suitable target date on which to adopt a new draft text centred on European criteria, rather than the situation at national level. A referendum on the Constitution could be held on the same day in all the Member States, making it clear that the political construction of Europe is more important and more urgent than national crises, for the simple reason that it can help to resolve them.

However, there are a number of major European political decisions which the Heads of State and Government could now take at the forthcoming European Council meetings, in the absence of the Constitution, for example to make their debates public, finally revealing how decisions are made. They could also decide to give European national parliaments a say in European laws, bringing deliberations at national and European level closer together. Thirdly, and finally, the Council does not need the Constitution to implement the right of petition, which would be a major step forward in democratic terms. These are three specific proposals which, if taken up before the end of the year, would at least display a will on the part of European leaders to make progress.

In particular, Europe must show that it is able to act and initiate Community policies. We have a common agricultural policy, so why do we not have a common policy in the field of research and innovation, without which we will never catch up with the United States and Japan? We have introduced the euro but have no prospect of economic and industrial coordination. Concerning energy autonomy, defence and foreign policy, who can deny that in a world of giants everything must happen at European level and that new common policies must be introduced here also?

The task facing us is immense, but not impossible, requiring a level of personal commitment in the European governments equal to that shown by the Prime Minister of Luxembourg, Jean-Claude Juncker.

Such a degree of commitment is necessary for us, since it is only by acting together that Europe and France can rebuild. It is also necessary for the world as a whole. During the summer, one man summed matters up extremely well, saying that "the world needs Europe as a demonstration that intelligence, reason and good will are stronger than historical fate". That man was Bill Clinton.

Once again, let us get down to work! Time is of the essence.

Antonio Di Pietro MEP

In every-day speak, the term 'globalisation' seems to have become one of those buzzwords meaning both everything and nothing at the same time. Think about your understanding of globalisation, and compare it with the meaning associated with 'democracy' throughout the world, in different political cultures and societies. You can easily figure out the risk of misinterpretation or, better, of a plurality of interpretations, for such a complex concept embedded in a simple thirteen letter combination!

The confusion is amplified by the hypertrophic and inflationary growth of books, theories, fora, workshops, conferences at any level in which everybody, from the renowned scholars to the last-minute amateurs struggle to prove they have got the "plug-and-play" formula to explain everything! Quantity seldom matches quality, but nevertheless such a wide production is a useful indicator for a first assessment of the importance people give this topic: googling 'globalisation' on 18th October, 2005 gives you 14,800,000 entries, to be added to the over 50 million you get if you try with 'globalization'. This is the same magnitude as the results you get with other words with a broader spectrum of application such as the roughly 230 million results for 'sex' and 'peace' or the almost $1/2$ billion for 'love' and 'war'. Globalisation gives even more results than 'unemployment' (44 million), 'global warming' (about 30 million) or 'famine' (a mere 11 million)! This simple exercise give us a first idea of how sensitive the issue of globali(s/z)ation is in our society.

That multiplicity of meanings of 'globalisation' is also often linked to the fact that the cognitive functions of human beings (opinion leaders are human beings too) are more focused on the 'product' (the perceived effect of globalisation) than on the 'process' (the phenomenon itself), since it is the effects of globalisation that we feel directly - just in the same way you can't see the microwaves of an oven but you see the food inside is being cooked - and you don't even need to be an expert on electromagnetic propagation to push the 'start' button!

Therefore, before even starting any would-be serious discussion on globalisation and in order to avoid risking this brief essay being the copy-paste of another's, I should point out what my personal understanding of globalisation is.

First of all, globalisation is a natural phenomenon of self-organisation of what is called, in another misused term, the 'global village'. It is one of those great forces of history which changed the world's economic, social and political structure, just like prehistoric migrations, the advent of agriculture, the industrial revolution or the IT revolution we're still experiencing. The driving forces are so widespread, deeply rooted, stratified and their mutual relationships and interdependencies so complex that it's hard to fully explain them. Taking that into account, it's obvious that even thinking about u-turning these kinds of processes is pure science fiction.

By the way, why should anyone counter globalisation? Globalisation is neither 'bad' nor 'good' by itself; it is simply a matter of fact. Nevertheless, globalisation certainly needs to be governed.

Globalisation is a phenomenon that comes with risks and, as everybody knows, risks entail both opportunities and threats. Good governance maximises the exploitation of the windows of opportunity offered by globalisation and mitigates the unwanted effects that might affect certain categories of people in certain areas of the world.

The enabling role of truly free world-wide economic competition is, in my opinion, the key area for understanding which concrete policies we have to put in place and which lines of action to promote as a 'world political class' in order to achieve a world net social benefit out of this extraordinary process.

More specifically, I'll concentrate my brief analysis on the following main pre-requisites:

- Globalisation has to go hand-in-hand with democracy, otherwise free economic competition cannot be achieved.

- This competition cannot be achieved if free off-shore paradises or enclaves for money laundering are tolerated.

Improving democracy

Although the term 'democracy' can be defined in many ways, we can assume the level of democracy is given by the 'mix' of widespread moral imperative throughout society and by the way social and political processes are organised.

This is not the right forum to start a philosophical and anthropological discussion on whether the widespread improvement of living standards has brought about a more favourable ground for developing those civic virtues upon which liberal democracy as a moral imperative is based. So, to keep it very basic, no free market economy can be established where there is insufficient protection of human rights and civil liberties. Let's imagine a country where formal (and sometimes extreme) freedom of establishing and running business is not matched by the people's (direct or indirect) syndicate control of the mechanisms regulating market transactions. How can continuity of business be achieved in those countries where not even individuals are protected by the rule of law and where democratic control of the judiciary is absent? Who will question the legitimacy of measures taken in favour (or against) one industrial group where not even the right of free speech is guaranteed? How can those segments of society subject to social and economic dumping express their need for redistributive policies where no specific instruments for the articulation of widespread common interests are available?

In this respect, the tumultuous development of China and the disturbances in the oil industry in Russia are visible and well known to the international public. Nevertheless, 'Western' countries are by no means immune from this danger, where it is still possible for a Prime Minister to use his legislative power to promote his and his friends' own financial interests…any possible reference to Italian current affairs is not unintentional!

Zero tolerance for off-shore fiscal paradises

We have recently witnessed much improvement in the field of free movement of some economic factors, mainly capital and, with some obvious limitations, labour. But sometimes capital, instead of migrating to where the local conditions are most suitable for a more efficient use of the capital itself, becomes a sort of virtual commuter from one State to another, with the sole objective of escaping taxation, disguising from the authorities the origin of the money itself. This huge and largely uncontrolled flow of money has many negative effects on the behaviour of the world market economy, by introducing artificial distortions in specific sectors or countries.

Although ambitious programmes against money laundering such as the UN's (GPML) aim to eliminate dirty money from the global economy, there is still much room for improvement (if we want to use 'improvement' as an euphemism). As far as the EU is concerned, the following considerations merit special attention[1]. For example, no attempt has so far been made at EU level to define precisely the term 'financial crime', which is comprised of a significant number of specific types or sub categories of crime. I firmly believe that deliberately hiding the origin of otherwise lawfully earned capital to evade legitimate control by the appropriate authorities is a criminal act. Paradoxically, some countries' legislation even leads to the opposite result, by considering false declarations of a company's assets and liabilities as no more than a civil offence! The 25 uncoordinated national criminal and civil law provisions and regulatory measures in this field in the EU should be consolidated and elaborated at the EU level into an integrated approach towards more effective financial crime prevention and law enforcement.

While on the subject, places such as the Virgin Islands, or even some places in Europe, have been transformed from a tourist paradise to a paradise for international less-than-transparent *brasseurs d'affaires*. In this respect, I firmly believe that national legislation should forbid companies registered on the stock exchange to hold shares or otherwise manage or control companies with a seat in one of those so-called

---

[1] Cfr also COM(2004) 262 final, Brussels, 16.4.2004.

'paradises'. At the same time it should be forbidden for companies with a seat in such places to take control of companies listed on the stock market to avoid possible fraud.

The final goal of globalising both rights and obligations for the international community is in jeopardy unless serious efforts are made to improve democracy and create a truly free world market economy. I am proud to belong to the group of Liberals who idealise this goal.

Mojca Drčar Murko MEP

Ralf Dahrendorf once defined the developed part of the word at its peak in the twentieth century as a successful combination of three positive characteristics[1]. It was made up of economies that ensured the good life for a large number of people, societies that encouraged individualism and competition without destroying the smaller communities in which the individuals lived, and political programmes that inseparably linked the rule of law to principles of democracy.

The inhabitants of Western Europe and North America - the industrially advanced 'First World' was concentrated primarily in these two regions - in contrast to people in the 'Second World' ('real socialism') and the 'Third World' (the developing countries), had comparatively equal economic opportunities as well as a social framework in which civil societies were able to develop stimulating mutual relationships. All people, without exception, also had guaranteed political freedoms, which was the historic cumulative result of the class struggles that had lasted several decades and two world wars. One of the main causes of both these wars was the very conflict with the systemic inequality between individuals and societies.

However, this model, which gave rise to the idea of a united Europe, had its deficiencies. It excluded the populations of a large part of the rest of the world from the possibilities and opportunities it offered its own populations. The countries outside the circle of enlightened industrial societies, which were unable to participate in the international commodity market with the same instruments, were condemned to falling behind permanently. Prosperity was, in short, a privilege not achieved everywhere. The situation began to change significantly only due to the globalisation of capital markets and the expansion of the information revolution.

There are several causes behind the acceleration of the international economy at that time. The Cold War ended because the Soviet social

---

[1] Dahrendorf, R., 'A Precarious Balance: Economic Opportunity, Civil Society, and Political Liberty', *The Responsive Community*, 1995, 5, pp 4-30.

system imploded due to its lost economic vitality; the operation of multinational corporations successfully linked local activity to global management; and a reduction in the economic importance of nation states; as well as the emergence of productive forces in large Asian countries. Those documenting the economic history of humankind present the simultaneity of all these phenomena as an international economic stage that cannot be compared to anything else in history to date. Borders have not only lost their importance through the free movement of capital, but even more so through trade in products and services. Is this framework an historic opportunity for the consolidation of contemporary liberalism or is it an aggravating circumstance for it?

Possibilities offered and used

To those parts of the world, which until then were systemically lagging behind, globalisation offered at least the theoretical chance that the privileges of the developed world would also become available to them. It was logical to expect that the underprivileged parts of the world would seize the opportunity and seek ways to speed up development. The economic internationalisation that was accompanied by numerous other global phenomena (ageing populations in one part of the world and a demographic explosion in another, the global networking of crime, various types of fundamentalism, climatic change etc) shed additional light on the particularity of the First World model. It became vulnerable. It was all but impossible to hide from the consequences of globalisation. In this competitive world, in which financial markets reach across the borders of any country, all the economies are intertwined and subject to uncertainty due to the demanding rules of the game.

In short, the model which at its peak had the luck of squaring the circle by combining prosperity, social stability and the political freedom of individuals has become a less reliable promise for the future. Individual societies have found themselves amidst various influences that they do not control. The governments were to a lesser extent capable of keeping all the promises they had made. The population, either affected by the unpleasant consequences or fearing that they might be affected by them in the future, is gripped by a feeling of being under threat.

This was indeed a shocking realisation. Within developed societies different submodels of the welfare state, which had emerged on the basis of different historical experiences, mindsets, economic structures and competition traditions, started seeking new avenues. The different ways of addressing the issue of globalisation may be summed up as two distinct patterns: the Anglo-Saxon and the continental. The former established the philosophy of competition as the basis of the economic and social model in the 1980s, under the sway of the conservative right. The latter relied much more on the connecting role of the state - which was closer to the way most people in the continental part of Western Europe thought at the time - although it also adapted and changed. The former countries of the East brought a specific legacy to 21st century Europe, as their unsteady development and unstable political circumstances had given rise to hybrid development patterns that oscillate between the powerful interventionist role of the state and drastic liberal economic instruments.

Neither of the models has been successful enough in resolving the outstanding issues to make its adoption straightforward, although there are indications that the Anglo-Saxon model has gradually proved more flexible, and the model developed in some of the countries of the former East has resulted in higher growth rates. On the other hand, one cannot ignore the adverse side effects of this model of development: the emergence of a subclass that has lost touch with the majority of society, mass illiteracy, environmental and climatic changes caused by unreasonable behaviour and actions, crime, generations of young people without a real possibility of leaving the environment of marginalised minorities and so on.

Fear of an unpredictable future

No one was prepared for the vulnerability of the 'First World', least of all those inhabitants of developed Western Europe who were suddenly expected to accept considerable temporary restrictions of their security, prosperity and political freedoms. The possible consequences of the adjustments - e.g. the reduction of social welfare and the increase in social differences, which might be followed by a curbing of liberal freedoms and, in emergencies, even by authoritarian measures - has made the future murky.

Most likely out of fear for their existing rights, in parliamentary elections or similar ballots European voters frequently vote against political and economic solutions that usher in radical changes. The motives behind these rejections vary from case to case, especially between the former Western and Eastern Europe, while the fear of changes in the status quo is common to all.

The fear that things could get worse has therefore become the new framework for analysing the concept of 'crisis'. Taking into consideration recent history, such fears are nothing new. They are based on the experience of earlier generations who lived with the consequences of the collapse of the New York Stock Exchange on 29th October 1929. The social catastrophe precipitated by this collapse made it clear to people why social security had been such an important political programme ever since the Industrial Revolution. It provided protection against the vagaries of life including unemployment, accidents, disease and the hopelessness of waiting for old age without any income.

The 2005 defeat of Germany's Social Democrats was linked to the fact that at the time of the election the unemployment rate in the country stood at 9.3%, higher than in 1998 when the party came to power, and even higher than four years later, when the party won a second mandate by a narrow margin. It is possible to conclude that the mass unemployment from the period of economic depression in the 1930s was not just America's collective trauma but probably also Germany's. This is new. So far, the different scopes of authorities exercising monetary policies in Germany (also in the European Union) and the US have been explained in terms of two different but deeply rooted historical debates. The US Federal Reserve must monitor the stability of the currency while controlling employment by means of monetary measures. The other task is to tackle the political consequences of the trauma of the great collapse of the Stock Exchange and mass unemployment. By contrast, the obligations of the European Central Bank, just like the Bundesbank before it, are limited to measures aimed at preserving monetary stability. As the result of the monetary crisis in Weimar Germany currency stability was to date considered the main, if not the only, thing that the Germans expect from good economic management.

Catch up, overtake...

The former 'Second World' of Europe has not been any less affected than its 'First World'. Having joined the core of the most developed countries of the European Union, this 'Second World' expected a rapid expansion of the model of the Western European welfare state, political freedom and accelerated development. The expectations were high, and the disappointment after a year of EU membership was therefore predictable, even though some of the new members had considerably higher rates of economic growth than the old ones. Starting from much less favourable economic positions, they introduced radical tax policy instruments, from Anglo-Saxon theory, which had never before been implemented either there or in any other developed country. In all likelihood, these new EU members, faced with the disorder in state services, concluded that it was better to introduce a low tax rate and have a stable flow into state coffers than to have high tax rates and income on paper that could not be collected. It seems that the economic miracles end here as the societies of the former 'Second World' are also ageing, the systems of the welfare state are stretched to breaking point, the reforms of the pension system are inadequate, and the outlay for education and science do not meet needs.

By accident, due to the simultaneous parliamentary elections in Germany and Poland in October 2005, it became obvious that in both former 'worlds' there had occurred tectonic shifts, which were much more than routine changes of governments and generations. In Germany, both mass popular political parties left and right of the political centre, who had built the post-war social market economy, lost a great deal of trust. In Poland, particularly due to the personal interlocking of the major players, the closely-linked parliamentary and presidential elections foreshadowed a 'fourth republic', an internationally distrustful Poland, fixated with the past rather than the future.

Just as in Germany, voters in Poland decided not to make a break with the existing state of affairs but opted instead for a paternalistic social state. The latter does not only correct periodic market incongruities but creates facts that affect the operation of the market. The similar expansion of new 'statism', which the conservative government is introducing in Slovenia by intervening in the economy (increasing state shares even in companies quoted on the stock exchange), suggests that this may be a broader trend in the new EU countries. This is contrary to the fundamental liberal view that a freely functioning market limits the number of cases that have to be resolved by political intervention.

One of the many characteristics that should be analysed is also the declining interest of people in politics and influence over the course of events by voting in elections. The catastrophically low turnouts in the first elections for the European Parliament in 2004 (only a quarter of all eligible voters cast their ballots in Latvia and Slovenia) are also being reported from national parliamentary elections. The fact that 60 per cent of all eligible voters in Poland did not feel comfortable with the role of sovereign and did not vote in parliamentary elections is, in all likelihood, testimony to a shortage of attractive alternatives to the paternalistic, 'liberating' populism that set the tone of the campaign. It is at the same time a reflection of the broader phenomenon of political apathy in modern states.

The question is whether it is a trend of moving away from the ideals of modern liberalism as individual liberal principles are being abandoned and authoritarian (populist) solutions are being applied. Are there any historical comparisons?

Unemployment - the malady of civilisation

Ever since the beginning of the industrial revolution, the history of the world economy has been the history of impressive technological progress, an increasing global division of labour, and financial flows that have linked economies into a global system. At the turn of the twentieth century, the faith in the power of technical progress as the basis for the gradual political liberation of individuals was already universal and apparently unstoppable. Even Turkey and Russia, the last two autocratic regimes in the European system of states, had by 1914 taken definite steps towards establishing constitutional governments. It seemed that nothing could reverse globalisation, leaning on liberal values, any longer. But as early as the end of the first decade of the century, which was marked by the (to date) most extensive migrations of Europe's inhabitants, the optimistic views gave way to pessimism. Two particular reasons for this were the standstill reached by the globalisation of the economy and the fact that between the two world wars the ideas of liberalism collapsed throughout Europe, with the exception of a handful of countries (Great Britain, Sweden, Switzerland, Finland and Ireland). In the view of historians, one of the most shocking messages of the period from the beginning of the First World War until the end of the Second World War was simply the universal breakdown of the values and institutions of liberal civilisation.

In their struggle against economic stagnation after the First World War, which lasted until the end of the Second World War, countries defended themselves with protectionist measures, which suggest that they perceived the globalisation of the economy as an external threat. "The Great Slump destroyed economic liberalism for half a century", Eric Hobsbawm wrote in his work *Age of Extremes; the Short Twentieth Century* in 1994. The combination of mass unemployment, the collapse of the prices of agricultural products and the consequences of these two developments affected people greatly and undermined their faith in politics, while the absence of solutions within the framework of the old liberal economy further closed the dead-end street. Having found themselves in a predicament, countries gave precedence to social thinking - fearing an increase in the influence of extremist political factions - above economic thinking and defended themselves with protectionist tariffs. As the final consequence, the adoption of short term defence measures in individual countries undermined the existence of the global economy, whose overall stagnation spread even more rapidly in these circumstances.

A pervading danger - authoritarian solutions

In contrast to the first globalisation of one hundred years ago, individual nation states cannot now stop 21st century globalisation with separate protectionist measures, protective tariffs and restrictions of international trade. The way out of the crisis is not in the renewal of protectionism; quite the contrary, it lies in removing the obstacles to the globalisation of the economy. Yet the short term prospects in the transition period are not great. Mobility, flexibility, deregulation, etc. are political formulae covering broad semantic fields. They all require people in the former 'First' and 'Second' worlds to say goodbye to the certainty when planning their lives. The mid-term perspective is the creation of a large middle class that must adopt 'mobile' and 'flexible' thinking instead of expecting the state to help. This, however, is not only a routine political issue, but also one of culture and civilisation.

In some countries of the 'Third World' that participate in the world market according to more comparable standards as before, new models are emerging, aimed at linking economic growth to the social stability of societies and to guarantees with regard to political freedoms. They appear as competition to the European model and as challengers.

The Politics of Cultural Despair is the title of a book published a few years ago by the German author Fritz Stern[2]. He sought connections among writers from the turn of the twentieth century to prove how deeply-rooted resistance in Germany was to the changing world of the time, including resistance to the market economy and political democracy. Drawing on this book, Ralf Dahrendorf concluded recently that, despite the defeat of the politics of cultural despair after the Second World War and the triumphalism of the market economy, it is still possible to detect fears in Germany - the largest country of the European Union and the world's largest exporter - of opening borders within the global economy. This is due to the fact that the management of economic affairs is too reliant on the state. Similar conclusions could, in all likelihood, be drawn in France and the Netherlands, in the wake of the referenda on the European Constitutional Treaty - not to mention the new EU member countries, where the state still owns considerable assets and, also as an owner, intervenes in market relations.

What we are facing is not a totally predictable and necessarily better world, as it seemed to optimists at the turn of the 21st century. However, there is no reason for negativity either, provided Europe manages once again to link efficiency in the global competitive struggle to the values of liberal democracy. It is important to resist the populist simplification

---

[2] Stern, F., *The Politics of Cultural Despair* (1974).

that would open the door to authoritarian measures and break the consensus on the values of modern liberal individualism. In other words, the sovereignty of the masses must not destroy the sovereignty of individuals. There is no reason for the European Union, which has learned lessons from adverse past experiences, not to creatively combine the numerous advantages it has as an emerging global player while preserving the welfare state, adjusted to a true balance between contributions by individuals and its collective responsibility.

Antoine Duquesne MEP

The world is changing, and in this constantly evolving world there is one current of thought and action which has the advantage of remaining remarkably fresh: liberalism. This applies both to addressing the new structure of society, which is increasingly tending to transcend national boundaries, and to approaches to our own personal aspirations.

Indeed, the very principles that underpin liberalism are also those that are changing our world: calls for greater freedom, a desire for democracy, the profile of human rights, the need to trigger initiatives enabling us to respond to the fundamental aspiration for greater justice, and so forth.

Furthermore, it is the principles of liberalism which are at the heart of the process of building Europe, which should from now on enable us to strengthen the political union of Europe, to modernise Europe, and to make it more competitive and flexible, more democratic, bring it closer to its citizens, more effective and less bureaucratic. In short, these principles should enable us to overcome the recent setbacks it has suffered and to regain the fighting spirit of its founding fathers.

The models that succeed are those that meet our citizens' expectations. The most recent members of the European family certainly see that, and the same applies, even more so in fact, to those who hope to become members of that family one day. For them, freedom - to think, to act, to create and to develop - is not an empty word, and what political philosophy embodies that better than liberalism, which puts the individual at the heart of its concerns and aspires to give individuals the means to realise their potential by using their abilities to the full?

If there were a successful 'Plan B', we would know about it. I have to say that I do not know of one! History tells us that all attempts at other types of society have sooner or later resulted in failure, poverty, a chronic lack of freedom, tyranny or even war.

No adjectives, no complexes

Those who now seek to qualify liberalism by prefixing some adjective or other to it are mistaken in doing so. Either they have are insecure in their liberalism, or they wish to denigrate liberalism and cannot find another way of blaming it for all the ills of our planet.

There is no need to talk about 'social liberalism', because liberalism is essentially social in any case - people are at the heart of our concerns and we do not regard growth curves as having any intrinsic value. In fact, they only have any value insofar as they facilitate job creation, help to combat social injustice, provide food for those who are hungry and drink for those who are thirsty, promote research to create a better world, and so on.

Unless they are backed up by the wealth creation that makes it possible to deliver them, generous promises are simply illusory. Liberalism has nothing to do with selfishness, quite the opposite. Liberalism is about deeds, not words!

Surely there can be no point in talking about 'neo-liberalism' unless it is to denigrate liberalism and make it responsible for all the problems with which we are faced? In reality, liberalism is a way of thinking and acting which is spreading all over the world and to which those who do not benefit from it aspire most. I say this because liberalism states that the individual should have inalienable basic rights: the right to live safely as long as one respects the rights of all, the right to think and to express these thoughts freely, the right to freedom in one's private life, to possess goods, to participate in communal life and to draw up common policies.

Fundamentally reforming

In reality, and perhaps it is this that disturbs some people, liberalism is fundamentally about reform and opposes all forms of conservatism, whether on the right or on the left. Liberalism is the element of change that allows society to evolve. It is the fundamental values of liberalism that make it possible - in a wide range of situations and contexts, with greater freedom and in a spirit of solidarity - for men and women to tackle not only their personal problems but also those of the society in which they live. They are also able to take on the problem of an increasingly demanding world, a world in which it is vital for us actively to demonstrate our solidarity with the most disadvantaged, and to allow them to regain their taste for life and their dignity by helping them to develop rather than simply offering them aid.

In our globalised world liberal principles are vital if the order essential for the much-needed implementation of distributive justice is to prevail.

Only principles which respect freedom and encourage progress will enable the most disadvantaged to improve their lot in life. Transfers of activity will be inevitable, both within and beyond Europe. This of course implies an appropriate social response on the part of our very privileged societies, which if they are to continue to develop will have to remain at the front of the pack by investing in innovation and quality, and implement accompanying social measures to encourage retraining of our workforce.

For liberals, it is essential to face the future, which is very much the aim of the Lisbon Strategy, and to give priority to investment in education, training and research. Education and training allow every individual to realise his or her own potential and thus guarantees high quality development. Research is essential not only for us to maintain our current living standards but also for the world as a whole to progress and offer a more promising future for an increasing number of our fellow human beings, wherever they live.

An institutional model
Liberalism is increasingly becoming a universal feature of our institutions, whether in the form of guarantees offered to the public by parliamentary systems, the independence granted to the judiciary, or checks on the executive.

This model is being further developed at European level as each day passes, reflecting the spirit and the hopes of the founding fathers of Europe. This is evidenced not only by the ever-greater powers already being assumed by the European Parliament, but also by the democratic advances enshrined in the draft European Constitution.

If that Constitution is finally approved or if its principles are at least incorporated elsewhere, the European Parliament will, amongst other things, become the Council's co-legislator in a great many fields, most notably justice and home affairs. The Commission will have a greater responsibility towards the Members of the European Parliament, and the Council's activities will become more transparent, while a qualified majority voting system will facilitate decision-making. The right to petition the Parliament will be strengthened. The bottom line is that citizens' basic rights will be safeguarded by both judicial and quasi-judicial means.

In short, under the institutional model that we are advocating, the citizen will be at the heart of the integration process. Freedom and human rights are the motors of European action.

It is worth noting that this model is a source of fascination in other parts of the world where the aim - one that is still all too often largely a dream - is to secure institutions whose hallmark is democracy, solidarity and peace. This applies particularly in Latin America, where many states have firmly resolved to turn their backs on their history of dictatorship, tyranny and fascism, and to set up active democratic bodies at regional level.

Our values

Liberalism is deeply rooted in human behaviour. This means that for us tolerance, concern for others, the protection of human rights and respect for the secular state are universal values in the face of which personal beliefs and convictions must be set aside if the identity of each individual is to be preserved. These values should also be instilled in young people at school in order to encourage the development of a harmonious society based on mutual respect.

At the same time, liberals believe that there can be no success without work, and that we need to maintain the taste for success and the spirit of enterprise, the sense of challenge and of dynamism, the will to create and innovate, and the notion that freedom and safety go hand in hand. This is simply common sense. Anyone who seeks to deny this will simply stir up anxiety amongst our citizens and leave the door wide open to extremists.

So, for example, we regard the rule of law, respect for each individual's basic rights and the protection of private life as essential. We must equip ourselves with effective means of combating major crime, which does not respect national borders, be it terrorism, trafficking in human beings, arms or drugs, money laundering, and so on. Without such means, our citizens' basic rights themselves are at risk.

'No' to fanaticism

Here in Europe, the area of freedom, security and justice that we are gradually establishing is the only way effectively to meet this challenge while continuing to respect each individual's rights and freedoms.

Terrorism poses a constant threat to democracy. Liberals are spearheading judicial and police cooperation not only within the Union but also with all those throughout the world who reject acts where perpetrators attack innocent people in the name of their fantasies and their fanaticism. There can be no justification for this.

We consider that it is vital to develop a strategy that is both preventive and reactive, on the basis of cooperation between Member States and the police and education authorities, in order to take action in relation to all those factors that are cited by way of justification for such acts, to educate public opinion with regard to democracy and the terrorist threat, and to seek to maximise effectiveness while respecting the rule of law.

We liberals firmly support a proactive approach to all the current forms of terrorism. It is essential to protect our societies' vital infrastructure, to halt the financing of terrorism and to significantly improve exchanges of information, whilst above all not forgetting the victims.

The tragic events in New York, Casablanca, Madrid and more recently in London demonstrate that this fight is a just and essential one, and is now of greater relevance than ever before.

Lastly, with regard to immigration, we must demonstrate that we are open, welcoming and conscious as regards the troubles afflicting our world. However, offering asylum to those at risk does not mean that we are willing to undermine our own culture and basic convictions.

The fox and the hen house

Freedom is increasingly becoming the hallmark of today's world: walls are coming down, those who are most disadvantaged are finally starting to see a way out of their plight, a willingness to enter into dialogue is replacing conflict, and markets are becoming ever more accessible. Contrary to what some may claim, liberalism is the only way of arranging the various mechanisms involved while guaranteeing the necessary flexibility and competition.

However, the freedom we stand for is not the freedom of the fox who gets into the hen house! Liberals do not advocate unbridled capitalism of the kind that flourished at times in the 19th century, and we believe that the world cannot be governed by the laws of finance alone. Quite the contrary, we believe in responsible freedom, with the State taking a regulatory role. You cannot simply do whatever you want wherever and however you wish. Total freedom would risk sowing the seeds of its own destruction. Freedom is limited by laws which are founded on rational analysis, which are known to all and which are consciously accepted. The State watches over these laws and ensures that they are respected. In a liberal and democratic state, the power of the State itself is checked by parliamentary representatives elected under universal suffrage. State intervention is limited to necessary and well-defined functions: this is known as the 'just state'.

For this reason, thanks to liberal values, Europe is now seen as the focal point of democracy and human rights. We should not feel any sense of superiority because of this but should in fact be aware of the responsibilities this implies not only towards our own citizens but also towards the rest of the world.

Even if European societies have made great progress by choosing liberalism, they cannot afford to rest on their laurels: this success could soon turn to dust if they do not have the will to meet challenges and take stock with a view to relentlessly pursuing modernisation.

When considering the draft European Constitution, this is the fundamental question that must be addressed, in addition to the text itself. Liberalism is not a 'little blue book' of practical formulas set in stone. No, rather it calls for constant and unrelenting efforts to achieve progress for humankind.

As long as Europe's decision-makers are not lured by the siren call of a certain political fashion, be it called 'altermondialism' or any other name, and remain proud of their liberal commitments, which are not the sole preserve of any one party and have brought us such success up to now, they will open up a future of hope in a difficult and troubled world.

Liberal Democrat summit before Hampton Court Council, October 2005. *From L to R: Finland's Prime Minister Matti Vanhanen, ALDE Leader Graham Watson MEP, Liberal Democrat Leader Charles Kennedy MP, Estonia's Prime Minister Andrus Ansip, ELDR Party President Annemie Neyts MEP, Belgium's Prime Minister Guy Verhofstadt, Denmark's Prime Minister Anders Fogh Rasmussen.*

The ALDE Group in support of Bronislaw Geremek MEP, candidate for the Presidency of the European Parliament, July 2004.

Annemie Neyts MEP and Graham Watson MEP await Liberal Democrat
Prime Ministers at Hampton Court summit, October 2005.

The ALDE Group meet the Council of Asian Liberals and Democrats,
November 2004

The ALDE Group at work, Autumn 2005.

Liberal and Democratic Leaders gather before the June 2005
European Council.

UDF Leader François Bayrou, European Commission President Romano Prodi
and Graham Watson MEP, March 2004.

The ALDE Group occupy the central block of seats in the hemicycle
in Strasbourg.

Lena Ek MEP

The world is facing enormous challenges. Wars and internal conflicts cause death, injuries and environmental damage. Poverty in all parts of the world causes diseases, starvation and many refugees. Lack of democracy and human rights abuses condemns millions of people to a life where they are in the hands of dictators. Environmental abuse destroys the air and contaminates the soil and water thereby making it impossible to live a healthy life or even to inhabit certain parts of the planet. Modern liberalism with its combination of respect for the individual, enhancement of human rights and belief in a market economy has a great responsibility and provides solutions and possibilities to these challenges.

A modern liberal industrial policy seeks to combine environmental concerns with social responsibility and economic growth. Sustainable development therefore needs a strong liberal force, not only in Europe, but on a global level. Industry needs to take its responsibility but there is also a strong need for a political driving force that has the courage to take necessary decisions.

Trade has throughout history proven to be a strong tool to change for the better and, to be honest, also for the worse. Therefore it is essential to have a discussion about the implications of trade. Trade provides for more effective allocation of resources, diffusion of knowledge, technology and new production methods, larger markets and greater competition. Trade barriers in richer countries can easily be used to make other countries poorer but in a developing country might also be used to strengthen the internal economy. India has for a long time restricted imports of cars in order to strengthen the national car industry while American and European trade barriers have been used to enforce a better economic situation for their own industry.

A recent World Bank study sees impressive overall welfare gains from successful multilateral trade liberalisation. The EU enlargement process is a very good example of this. Trade barriers are detrimental to economic development but reform has to be more sensible than that. It has to evaluate the consequences not only for trade and industry in general, but for trade and industry in specific circumstances in various parts of the world.

Opening an economy to trade also means exposing it to information and other new influences. Consequently, trading in China brings forward a balance between concern for human rights, environmental hazards and economic considerations. The Chinese government is trying to restrict information from abroad but trading means that people need to have access to the Internet. Thus, even if the Internet is censored, there is still a possibility for information to be distributed among the Chinese people. Those who were in contact with people living behind the Iron Curtain realise how important this is. Information about other societies, human rights and democracy proves that there are alternative ways of living and provides an opportunity to form an opposition.

Spatial planning, or rather the lack of it, turns rural economies into economies centred around cities or even mega-cities. This causes huge environmental problems, which get worse every minute. In Hong Kong you cannot, even on a clear day, see the ancient tourist attractions through the film of air pollution. The ground water level is sinking dramatically in some parts of China. And as for Europe, around the major cities it is not wise to feed your baby ground water because pollution restricts the development of the kidneys of a growing child. In other areas the soil is contaminated by chemicals and impossible to use for many years. Therefore, production and industry policies have to be combined with high environmental and social standards. The recent proposal for a chemicals regime in Europe, the draft 'REACH' directive, provides for the registration, evaluation and authorisation and eventually substitution of dangerous chemicals and will hopefully provide balanced legislation to deal with such challenges.

Energy for development

The politics of energy become more and more important. Energy is power. The world market has in recent years experienced the effects of growing demand in China. However, we have not yet seen the effects of an expanding industry on the global energy market, and the ever-expanding number of consumers in China, South America and India. Furthermore, the melting of the Polar ice caps, resulting in rising sea levels, has spurred a completely new debate in the United States. At the same time organisations such as the CIA are publishing reports on security issues closely linked to the energy question.

Moreover, energy is under debate in the United States after the natural disasters that have occurred during 2005 (for example hurricanes Katrina and Rita). It is noticeable that President Bush has declared major American investment in research into alternative fuels. This has already begun in common research projects carried out by the major universities and research centres. China has also invested in alternative energy sources, research and development. And there will be more to come.

In Europe many countries are heavily dependent on imports from Gulf countries. At least ten of the twenty five EU nations are highly dependent on Russia for their energy. A substantial proportion of German industry looks to Russia for its gas supply. President Putin recently assured Europe that Russia will supply its energy demand, but many European decision makers are not entirely happy with this prospect.

Research for the Future

Knowledge is power. This is clear from historic experience, both when it comes to the fight for freedom, the fall of the Berlin Wall, but also with regards to economic development. In today's world, knowledge and cooperation, the so-called 'soft powers', are the way to change societies. That is why the United Nations, in talks about the Millennium goals, stresses the importance of knowledge and emphasises the importance of educating women.

With an overall sluggish economic performance in the European Union a change is definitely needed! More than five years ago, with complete consensus, the European Council set the Lisbon Agenda as the overall guideline for European policies. "In 2010, Europe shall be the most dynamic, knowledge-based economy in the world"[1].

---

[1] March 2000, agreement of EU Heads of States and Governments.

These are daring and inspiring words. The background is well known, but merits repeating. During the 90s the US economy boomed as never before in peacetime, leaving Europe far behind and reminding many of us of Jean-Jacques Servan-Schreiber's *The American Challenge*[2] - a book which profoundly impacted upon European policies several decades ago. In the last few years we have learned that Europe is not only facing a competitor in America, but also increasingly so in Asian economies, and certainly not forgetting Brazil. On the other hand, policies on national as well as on EU level, are sluggish and lack vision. In order to achieve the goals of the Lisbon agenda by 2010, the European economy - as we know from the half time report of Wim Kok[3] - needs the very opposite. And a miracle to go with it.

The growth of the EU-25 in comparison to that of the US and Japan is not faring well. With its poor economic performance Europe is even more vulnerable to any fluctuation in the global economy. Competition is getting fiercer. Thus, it is of vital importance to see that Asia is not competing with T-shirts, rice and simple plastic buckets produced by cheap labour. On the contrary, Asian economies are at an increasing pace developing high technology products, supported by very strong investment in Research and Development. When it comes to such investment on the other side the Atlantic, the American economy speaks for itself.

High level research is increasingly complex and interdisciplinary. It is costly. And it requests a constantly expanding 'critical mass'. No research teams, no single university and no company can create these conditions on their own. Not even one Member State of the European Union is releasing sufficient resources to plan and conduct complex research projects alone. Modern research in a global world needs cooperation, networking and mobility, both of individuals and ideas.

In this context the added value of a European Framework for research policy is obvious. The proposed Seventh Framework Programme for Research is ambitious, calling for a doubling of the European research

---

[2] Servan-Schreiber, J., *The American Challenge* (1967).

[3] http://europa.eu.int/growthandjobs/pdf/kok_report_en.pdf. (Accessed 1st November 2005).

budget. It proposes cooperation within four different cross-thematic approaches, designed to gain leadership in key scientific and technological areas and the establishment of an independent European Research Council that will support creativity and excellence in European science. However, the problem is that the governments of Europe have chosen to engage in quarrels about budgetary problems instead of seeing the overall picture - the need for a knowledge-driven economy to boost competitiveness and economic growth!

Economic growth to pay for an environmental and social agenda

Liberals truly believe that economic growth is needed in order to combine environmental interests and a genuine social agenda, building on human rights and democracy. The Lisbon Council identified research as the single most important tool for long term dynamic economic and social development in Europe. The Commission proposal quickly became a beacon of optimism in European policies. A large number of industrialists and scientists are engaged in preparations for its implementation. It signals a strong belief in the future for a European knowledge-based industry and thus for growth and jobs. The United Nations Millennium goals outline what has to be achieved when it comes to fighting poverty and reaching high environmental standards, as well as in terms of democracy and human rights. These are supported and made real by liberal politicians all over the world.

The single market in Europe has significantly raised Europe's economic potential. But more has to be done. Openness to trade and investment has been a catalyst for growth.

Today there are more than 60,000 global multinational companies. There are standards such as the OECD (Organisation for Economic Cooperation and Development) ethical guidelines, the ILO (International Labour Organisation) conventions and recommendations as well as the UN Global Compact initiative to ensure that companies as well as politicians follow an ethical framework in business, production and trade. There are rules for areas such as policies, information, worker protection, child labour, environment, corruption, consumer interests, research, competition, risk capital and taxation. These initiatives, especially Kofi Annan's 'Global Compact', need and deserve our full support as this is one way to achieve the sustainable economic development that we want!

The European challenge

The 'no' votes in France and the Netherlands on the proposed Constitutional Treaty left the European Union in confusion over its own future. When the negotiations over the Financial Perspectives broke down in June 2005 the gloom thickened significantly. It was as if even the European leaders had lost faith in the European project. But Europe needs visions, leadership and hope more than ever. The value of European cooperation must be clearly shown to the citizens - we need to give value to voters.

In addition, Europe has a responsibility for global development. Thus, it is of great importance how we choose to act in the WTO or the OECD negotiations, the way we work with human rights and democracy in the United Nations and the way we implement a common agenda in Europe. We have colleagues with liberal values all over the world. Our cooperation and engagement can provide a solution to many of the global problems. I have tried to show this in industrial policy and when it comes to sustainable economic growth, but it is indeed true in all political fields.

This will not be easy, but it is crucial. It is no longer time for formal speeches, now it is time to start delivering. And the liberal agenda has many of the answers needed!

Jelko Kacin MEP

A few years ago I visited the People's Republic of China for the first time. I remember being full of inspiration and sincerity, I would speak openly and directly as a true defender of human rights. Despite the fact that I come from a country populated by just two million people I found myself tempted to give advice to politicians governing a country with 750 times more people than my own. I came down to earth quickly when I was told that everything is relative in this world and that there is not and cannot be only one truth. My hosts held that the biggest achievement of their democracy is the extermination of hunger. I realised that the right not to be hungry could be the fundamental human right. For those who have experienced hunger this could be an enormous and historical achievement, but for us, in the developed part of Europe, this is an ascetic approach, which we need to have pointed out to us - and even then many Europeans have trouble understanding this message. We are not sensitive and attentive enough to other people who are different and different-minded. We are convinced that Europe is the centre of the world when this is simply not true. There are many other, different and equally important people, cultures, and civilisations in the world. We Europeans are the primary victims of our Eurocentricity which makes it so difficult for us to see the world as it really is.

Being liberal and libertarian is a big challenge for us all, requiring argument and confirmation every day. Some while ago I received a thank you note after I wrote to congratulate the newly elected President of the Liberal Democrats of Bosnia and Herzegovina, Dr. Lamija Tanovi. It prompted me to wonder what liberalism and libertarianism means for politicians and the public in an exhausted, demolished, multinational and multicultural country which has many different religions, and survived so many horrific experiences such as the Srebrenica massacre.

The note read as follows:
"Liberal Democrats of Bosnia and Herzegovina need to follow the road which you, our Slovenian friends, have already successfully embarked on. We sincerely hope that you will help us as true friends.

The European path is our priority and all our future political actions will be directed towards this. Your knowledge and help will be invaluable to us, because this makes us different from other political options - affiliation to a European political family which is ready to help and work hard for the development of liberal ideas everywhere where this is especially difficult".

Can liberalism also mean forgiveness and reconciliation? Is there a liberal and libertarian position of some Member States, such as Austria, Hungary, Slovakia, and Slovenia who support the opening of Croatia's accession negotiations without delivering the Hague-indicted General Gotovina? Croatia cannot receive a date to open negotiations, as long as she fails to fulfil her obligations. General Gotovina is not the only problem. 70% of Croatians believe Croatia will not get a date for some time. People are more realistic than politicians - they know what kind of changes Croatia is ready for and they are still not ready to hand over Gotovina. Ten years on from the horrific massacre in Srebrenica, it is impossible to convince a politician from the Netherlands to open negotiations before war criminals are handed over.

The experience of the Dutch battalion under the flag of UN in Srebrenica is far too bitter for the whole of Europe, especially those in the European Union, to risk making the same mistake again. In the case of Srebrenica there is not and cannot be any indulgence or forgiveness. Why was the court in The Hague established if not as a direct result of Srebrenica and other 'smaller Srebrenicas'? Is this a question of principle? Yes, it is about principles and civilisation standards in Europe and in the European Union. We ask ourselves why should Serbia hand over Generals Mladić and Karadzic to the Hague in order to get a date to open negotiations on a Stabilisation and Association Agreement, if Croatia can get a date to open accession negotiations without handing over General Gotovina. If we are both liberal and libertarian we cannot accept double standards.

These were my thoughts some months before the Council decision to open accession negotiations with Croatia on 3rd October. The Council's decision was a simple consequence of the Hague Chief Prosecutor Carla del Ponte's sudden decision that Croatia had finally begun fully cooperating with the ICTY (International Criminal Tribunal for the Former Yugoslavia). However it is now up to Croatia to prove this cooperation through successfully mastering the negotiation process, which also includes the issue of General Gotovina. The sooner Croatia solves this problem, the sooner it will be able to hand over the General to the Hague. This will enable Croatia to close a number of the most complicated chapters of the negotiations.

It would be a catastrophe if in the future the Chief Prosecutor were to establish that Croatia is again not fully cooperating with the ICTY. This would be especially bad for Croatia, but also for all those involved, including the ICTY. It would also negatively affect the process of peace and forgiveness in the Western Balkans. I say this as a warning to all the countries of the Western Balkans and also to all those involved in the EU decision-making and enlargement process. Non-cooperation by Croatia would potentially affect all the current and future candidate countries, the European Parliament, Commission, Council, Member States and the opinion of the wider European public. For this reason I look forward to full cooperation between Croatia and the Commission.

This is also the starting point for further enlargement of the EU. Without a breakthrough of liberalism and libertarian thinking, Bulgaria, Romania, and Turkey wouldn't be able to make the deep and rapid changes which has helped bring them so close to EU membership. Turkey's position in Europe must be approached with flexibility. Europe is different and bigger following the fall of the Berlin Wall. But even prior to that Turkey was on the Western and democratic side. Turkey has made great progress on this side in the last few years and for decades protected our world. The political élite of the United States has never looked at the world from a European perspective - even today they continue to view the world differently. At the same time they continue to remind us of the role and importance of Turkey in the peace, stability and security of Europe. When it comes to geopolitics, American involvement can be useful and this is certainly the case when it comes to Turkey. The economic consequence of the EU extending to Turkey is a difficult question. To me, as a new member of the European

Parliament, the realisation that sooner or later everything boils down to the Common Agriculture Policy (CAP) and subsidies was invaluable.

Liberalism and libertarianism also requires us to declare our position on untouchable dogmas, such as CAP. On the eve of the British Presidency of the EU, Tony Blair prepared to abolish the British Rebate in exchange for France conceding the untouchable CAP. The CAP is not policy but dogma. As long as we remain hostage to dogmas in the EU, we will not be able to accelerate progress. The new Member States are well aware of the need for a new decision-making process, as proposed by the EU Constitutional Treaty, which replaces monopolies and vetoes with equality and egality. France stands as the most ardent opponent of this. Whatever Blair achieves in this matter is both his and our success. London has already proved that it does not yield to the extension of European dogmas. At the same time a 'no' to the new financial perspective is not (yet) a catastrophe because the argument concerns only one per cent of the Gross National Product (GNP) of the EU making most money in their coffers. An agreement can be reached for this very reason. There are countries in Europe, such as Denmark, where even politicians can be heard quietly muttering that their farmers will survive the abolition of subsidies. On the other hand, there are countries in Latin America and Africa, which can offer nothing to the EU, except their agricultural products. If we do not liberalise our market, what can we offer them? The EU continues to destroy agriculture in African countries through the subsidies it offers to its own farmers. This surely cannot stand as an example nor an illustration of liberalism.

I have heard it said that Turkey has more farmers today than the entire EU put together. However, we have to face the globalisation and dilemmas facing the World Trade Organisation. Cancun is still vivid in our memory and new WTO Director General Pascal Lamy will have to again persuade the EU to confront the issue of agriculture. After all, isn't the question of sugar in the EU above all a question of privileges and monopolies which must be surrendered to the benefit of producers and suppliers from less developed countries? The number of farmers in Turkey will, after all, decrease in the future. The EU's enlargement to Turkey cannot and should not be hostage to the interest of those Member

States which still demand the same share of agriculture subsidies as they received when they were less developed.

Turkey has already proven that it has a dynamic economy with huge potential and that it can quickly adapt, offering quality products and services at competitive prices. Companies which grow, survive, and I believe that the EU and Turkey can perform better in the world market as one entity rather than separately. In the latter case I am less concerned about Turkey's economy, although I am convinced that both would benefit from Turkey's accession to the EU. I believe that the inclusion of Turkey presents the EU with numerous opportunities in the world market and globalisation process. Together with Turkish entrepreneurs we can contribute much to the development of other economic entities in Central Asia, thus making the EU's neighbouring regions more stable and friendly both locally and globally.

What would Turkey's accession bring to the EU? For certain the EU would gain one more official language - Turkish. This is something the EU already anticipates since it should have been joined by Cyprus together with the Turkish community in the north of the island but, due to opposition from the Greek Cypriots, this has not yet happened. In my opinion this was a major historical mistake. By recognising Turkish as an official EU language we could contribute more to the speed, depth and content of the negotiations and modernisation of Turkey than with negotiations which have not even started yet. Millions of Turks at home and throughout Europe could discover, examine and accept the rules and requirements of the EU on the Internet, which would strengthen and deepen the process of democratisation in Turkey. The old EU Member States do not pay enough attention to the role and importance of the use of one's mother tongue in the accession process because they are less aware of the sensitive nature of national identity and equality in transitional countries. Politics is of greater importance in transitional regimes than in old democracies where a high level of political apathy is often present. Language is the prime and main stimulus of development for societies in transition.

Turkey already has a delegation in the Parliamentary Assembly of the Council of Europe where Turkey's Foreign Minister Gul, a great liberal friend of the EU and a sincere advocate and campaigner for accession to the EU and the related changes in Turkey, has been very active. According to the current rules of the game Turkey will probably be under-represented for her size.

The EU was able to give a positive answer to Turkish expectations on 3rd October 2005 by opening accession negotiations. Turkey is already changing and, in the process, so is the entire EU. Many hope that Turkey will fail in its path to the EU, but it will not. Turkey will be able to deal with all the traumas of its past and the country will change so much that it will make us all proud and, in certain instances, also set us an example.

If we look further than our backyard we will be stronger, taller and we will see many things which we are unable to today. We will see Turkey and behind and next to it other states and nations belonging to our world which will become bigger and better, and future-oriented. When I was born, visionaries could see beyond the here and now resulting in the conception of the European Coal and Steel Community. I was born in Yugoslavia, a state that no longer exists, and without moving I now live in another, different, better and bigger world. In the EU today there are many more of us - I live with former enemies and yet I do not feel threatened. On the contrary, I feel safe and I look forward with confidence to our children's' future.

Silvana Koch-Mehrin MEP

Globalisation is first and foremost a good thing. It has, however, been blamed for much - from child labour to environmental destruction and many other ills in our society. Everyone seems to have something to say, be it anti or pro-globalisation. Yet there is a pronounced lack of knowledge about how globalisation operates and what it has achieved to date.

Globalisation has enriched many aspects of our everyday lives. And more to the point, it has profound ethical dimensions. Opposition to globalisation can be attributed to ignorance and myopia. Globalisation is the most powerful source of social good in today's world and often helps alleviate many of the problems for which it has been blamed. Poverty, women's rights, wage and labour standards, the environment and democracy worldwide are all positively affected by globalisation.

There are many who believe that globalisation increases economic prosperity in the conventional economic sense of 'enlarging the pie'. But others believe that charges brought against it range from it weakening the war on poverty, the assault on gender discrimination and the failure to protect culture. In the eyes of its critics, multinational corporations embody the socially destructive side of globalisation.

Globalisation constrains national sovereignty and hence limits the sense and scope of democratic control. Actions taken by one European Union Member State or their trade partners naturally affect others. It can also be argued that globalisation promotes the transition of autocratic regimes to democracy. Thus, interestingly, globalisation seems to apparently promote democracy while simultaneously constraining it. But how does this work?

Economic prosperity produces a wealthy middle class. The emerging middle class creates an effective demand for the democratisation of politics: the newly-created bourgeoisie seeks a political voice. Against this backdrop, globalisation leads to prosperity and this in turn leads to democratisation of politics through the rise of a middle class.

Bill Clinton has argued that as the Chinese become more mobile, prosperous, and gain awareness of alternative ways of life, they will seek greater say in the decisions that affect their lives. There is strong evidence that economic prosperity, engineered through globalisation, embodied by economic freedoms and use of market forces rather than central planning, promotes democracy. With this in mind it is interesting to contrast the Russian and Chinese experiences.

Russia - or at that time the Soviet Union - under Mikhail Gorbachev opted for glasnost, (political freedom and democracy) before perestroika (economic restructuring). In contrast China opted for economic change without an accompanying democratisation process. China's enormous success and Russia's devastating failure have led to the belief that democratisation should not precede economic reforms. Instead, economic reforms, resulting in prosperity and a wealthy middle class, will ultimately lead to democratisation. However, this isn't a case of 'one size fits all' - each case needs to be dealt with on an individual basis.

EU enlargement - small scale globalisation

Globalisation not only affects distant societies such as Russia and China, it also affects us here in Europe. At the beginning of the 21st century, the European Union and its Member States face the challenge of taking responsibility for a new security order on the European continent. To be more precise, it is not a new order that is being developed; merely expanding existing Western organisations to the East. In the last century, the decline of the Soviet Union, the disappearance of the Eastern bloc and the 'Iron Curtain', as well as German reunification all offer us the chance to overcome the political and economical division on the continent for good. The Council of Europe has already admitted new members, as has NATO, and the European Union is planning for further expansion in the coming years. Romanian and Bulgarian MEPs already sit in the European Parliament, and are due to gain full membership in 2007.

This process of enlargement is led by the idea that by expanding the area of integration and zone of prosperity, as well as democracy and stability towards the East, lasting peace and freedom will follow. Yet the admittance of new Member States is not only a question of geographical and numerical expansion for the Union. Even if the enlargement is taken gradually, it will have significant consequences for the structure and mode of operation of the European Union. It will also be necessary to ensure the question of what European integration is ultimately seeking to achieve - and how soon that that goal can be realised. A European Union that cannot fulfil its promises, or that cannot deliver on expectations, will not be able to guarantee stability and enduring peace. Losing political efficiency on the one hand, and losing the confidence of the people on the other, would be devastating to the enlargement process.

The original institutions of the Union were designed around a membership of only six nations. Understandable concerns now surround the question of whether they can function as efficiently as required for twenty-five members rather than six. In the latest enlargement phase of 2004 barely any changes were made. What - and how much exactly - from the 'old structure' of the EU must be maintained, and what must be changed or created in order for it to stay politically effective?

The Union faces internal challenges of efficiency, legitimacy and decisiveness. But in terms of relations with the 'outside', the European Union faces new tasks as well. The frontiers of Fortress Europe have shifted with the admittance of new members, and will shift again.

The EU is a veritable melting pot of very different countries whose structures have developed in very different ways. Enlargement towards the East and the South will encompass even more differences. Once all candidate countries have joined the EU it will almost double the number of members, increase in area by about 34%, and increase in population by 100 million people (28%). Interestingly enough, it will mostly be the countries recently returned to democracy and market economy that will join - countries in which the process of this return will not be complete by the time of their accession. Overall, it is a very positive signal that they will trade their regained sovereignty so quickly to share it with other nations in the Union.

The difference in per capita income and prosperity in general is also very important. Cyprus, for example, has a per capita income of about 75% of the EU average, Bulgaria or Romania on the other hand only 25%. An enlarged European Union will be relatively poorer, and the discrepancies in wealth between the Member States will become more pronounced. Both sides cherish different expectations of EU enlargement. The ten Eastern and central European states wish to document their affiliation to the European people, a relationship they were kept away from during the time of communist rule. They also aspire to securing their political, economical and social transformation and, alongside this transformation, expect the European Union to continue their help and support during this process. The membership of a strong EU internal market and financial aid program, particularly in agriculture is perceived as an essential factor in participating in the growing affluence of Europe.

Nevertheless, the potential new members fear the prosperous and powerful EU countries as well: people already suffering as a result of the structural change believe that their situation will get even worse - a fear that is also felt by critics of globalisation. Generally, people fear they will be overpowered by stronger European countries and that their ageing technology will be unable to compete.

In long-standing Member States there exists growing concern that the vast differences in terms of wealth and economic potential might cause additional problems and pressures. This is partly illustrated by Germany and Austria, already struggling with high unemployment figures, who in particular fear a massive influx of cheap labour from new Member States that would result in an even more critical labour market.

Despite these concerns there can be no argument that the enlargement of the European Union - or globalisation to put it in the wider picture - is not the right thing to do. Through enlargement, dangerous political instability posing uncalculated risks to Member States can be avoided. By securing a common policy in terms of visas and asylum, immigration and the fight against organised crime (especially in the new Member States), security within the Union can be optimised. Germany, for example, has shown very early that support for stable, strong and trustworthy countries beyond her borders and that EU enlargement may well be the best way to achieve this. Furthermore, the members of the European Union today anticipate the countries playing catch-up will, during their process of economic growth, stimulate the industries of the old Member States - and by doing so also secure the wealth of these states.

In the light of such conflicting expectations, consensus among the population of the Member States declines - and the referenda in France and the Netherlands clearly illustrate this. Within the EU, less than 50% are in favour of the enlargement, and even within the applicant countries scepticism grows.

Consequently, governments on both sides are confronted with some serious problems regarding legitimacy. It would be very difficult to continue with the enlargement process if the majority of the population rejects it; and even worse, the stabilising effect of the enlargement would be at risk if the joining of an individual candidate could be prohibited by a referendum in the country.

Poland - Exporting Democracy

Let us take a closer look at Poland as an example of how globalisation works to benefit of liberal values. Although, geographically speaking, it is clearly a central European country, and the Poles have felt European for some time (interestingly, people in the 'West' had always counted Poland as being part of the 'East'), a real chance to unite with 'Western' Europe emerged late in 1989, as a result of the Solidarnosc movement and its success in transforming Polish politics and society.

Poland became the first country in central Europe in which Communists - after a 45-year rule - lost power after agreements between government and opposition and finally elections in June 1989. The first democratic government of central Europe under Tadeusz Mazowiecki soon followed its foreign policy objectives and started to discuss the first steps towards future membership of the European Union. That was no less important than the security of the fledgling democracy, for a chance of ongoing economic and social development was at stake.

The European Union did not hesitate to welcome the positive approaches made by Poland and began talks in autumn 1989. Together with the Czech Republic, Poland signed the European agreement, a regulatory framework for future membership in the European Union in December 1991. As an economic effect of this agreement, Poland and the EU obliged themselves to create a free trade area between both parties within ten years, which they succeeded in doing. At the same time, the PHARE programme (Poland and Hungary: Action for the Restructuring of the Economy), a financial aid programme, came into force. Slowly but persistently, Poland changed its laws and regulations to fit into the European Union membership requirements.

During the same period Poland signed a free-trade agreement with the states of EFTA, which - at that time - still included Austria, Sweden and Finland. Together with Hungary, Slovenia and the Czech Republic, Poland founded the "Central European Free Trade zone" (CEFTA), extending the same obligations between each other that the European Union had interwoven between its members. As further preparation for its membership, Poland started - together with the Czech Republic and Hungary - the negotiations for membership of the OECD in 1993 (Organisation for Economic Cooperation and Development). In 1994 Poland became a member of the World Trade Organisation (WTO) and by 1996 had become a member of the OECD. Application for the membership of the European Union was made on August 4th, 1994.

The European Union formulated criteria for admitting new Member States at a conference in Copenhagen in 1993. The most important factors were democracy and the rule of law, a functioning market economy, the ability to compete in the EU's internal market, the adoption of EU laws and regulations and the consent regarding the economic and fiscal policy as well as political union.

During the Luxembourg summit of 1997 the EU agreed to start preparations for Poland (and five other countries) to join. In that process, these countries were assessed on the progress they had made on the necessary arrangements and fulfilling the requirements. The screening looked at 29 points, divided into three so-called 'columns'.

The first column dealt with questions of economy, the second with foreign policy and security, the third with domestic policy and law. By late 2001 Poland had fulfilled 18 points of this agenda. Cyprus and Hungary by comparison had already fulfilled 23, Slovenia 20, Slovakia, the Czech Republic and Estonia 19. The example of Poland and the export of democracy to a country suffering under socialism and dictatorship, well illustrates changes which can be brought about by globalisation.

In conclusion, the arguments that globalisation will promote democracy are much more robust than those that say that it will impair its reach and efficacy. But nevertheless, there is criticism as well: it is said that politicians embrace globalisation even when the people oppose it. Are they therefore acting undemocratically?

Undoubtedly, there are problems created by globalisation. But by dwelling too much on them, we will miss the chance to emphasise the many chances and benefits that globalisation can bestow if it is directed wisely and effectively. Globalisation is essential for the spread of democracy. Now information is freely available to anyone at anytime, censorship and undemocratic leadership will not last. The bottom line is that globalisation liberalises the world.

Baroness Sarah Ludford MEP and Frendehl Sipaco Warner

"People empowered can demand respect for their dignity when it is violated. They can create new opportunities for work and address many problems locally. And they can mobilize for the security of others"[1].

Introduction

We hear a lot from the critics of globalisation. They argue that for many people, it is synonymous with economic and social dislocation resulting from vulnerability to unpredictable market and technological forces. The dark side of globalisation is the increased opportunities for criminality that freer movement and communications allow, such as drugs, arms and people trafficking as well as terrorism. The international spread of AIDS and SARS is also a consequence of increased travel.

But proponents of globalisation admire the rapid advance of cross-border economic integration, the spread of powerful information technology and the opening of new horizons and contact through travel, as an illustration of the success and irreversibility of the process of globalisation. Globalisation, however, is not limited to the cross-border flows of goods, services, capital, technology and labour. Ideas and information are also included in the globalisation process, and in the current 'global village' or 'world community', this has involved the dissemination of information on, and the promotion of, human rights.

This essay discusses globalisation as a political strategy and effective instrument in human rights observance and advocacy. It specifically focuses on the developments in global communications in recent years, and how these developments have contributed to the empowerment of human rights actors in their endeavours to protect and promote the rights of their 'global compatriots' or fellow human beings in different parts of

---

[1] Mary Robinson quotes the Commission on Human Security in a speech entitled *"Making Globalization Work for all the World's People"* 22nd July 2003, Aspen Institute Summer Speakers Series, Aspen, Colorado. Transcript of speech sourced from http://www.eginitiative.org (Accessed 4th October 2005).

the world. We look at globalisation 'through the prism of liberal ideas'[2] and see it as an emancipatory tool that facilitates global solidarity and the universality of human rights, and strengthens human rights observance and advocacy.

(Values-led) Globalisation as a human rights project: Civil society and human rights advocacy

"Without a humane face, globalisation accentuates existing gaps, posing in the process one of the most formidable obstacles to human dignity"[3]

The processes which have facilitated the increases in the mobility of people, capital, goods and ideas have created possibilities for new global networks in all areas of life. Economic and technological globalisation have not only created new living conditions, but a significant reduction in the spaces that have separated people in different parts of the world across traditional territorial borders[4]. Goods and services that are traditionally available only to wealthier countries can now be accessed in the Third World. Developments in air, land and sea travel have made it easier, faster and more affordable to travel from one part of the world to another. According to a 2003 report by the International Organisation for Migration[5], one out of every 35 people in the world are migrants[6]. Modern communication technologies have also altered subjective senses

---

[2] Watson, Graham. *2020 Vision - Liberalism and Globalisation.* Centre for Reform, London, 2001, p 88.

[3] Monshipouri, Mahmood and Welch, Claude. 'The Search for International Human Rights and Justice: Coming to Terms with the New Global Realities.' *The Human Rights Quarterly.* 23 (2001), pp 370-401 at 386.

[4] Jones, RJ Barry. *The world turned upside down? Globalization and the future of the state.* Manchester University Press, Manchester and New York, 2000, pp 9-10.

[5] International Organization for Migration. World Migration Report 2003. Sourced from the Internet, http://www.iom.int/DOCUMENTS/PUBLICATION/EN/chap01p1_24.pdf (Accessed 13th October 2005).

[6] While developments in travel have facilitated ease of movement, a number of different factors have contributed to increases in rates of migration, such as poverty, the fall of the Iron Curtain, ethnic violence and refugee crises, and human trafficking.

of time and space, generating a perception of a 'global village', and allowing the free flow of ideas and information across territorial, cultural and social boundaries.

At the same time, globalisation has also been associated with notions of community and responsibility in the context of a market-driven society, as reflected in Mary Robinson's 'Realizing Rights: The Ethical Globalisation Initiative'[7]. This is compatible with the social liberal recognition of the need for intervention and assistance in an imperfect market place to give disadvantaged individuals the means to fend for themselves[8]. This phenomenon has even been labelled by some theorists as the 'globalisation of democracy', involving the transmission of ideas and promoting democracy and human rights as the most legitimate method of governance and political order[9].

Values-led globalisation as a human rights project is led by global civil society. The concept of a global civil society is associated with cosmopolitan notions of a worldwide political community and universal human rights that transcend the sovereignty and territorial jurisdiction of nation states[10]. Civil society is promoted by liberals as an effective engine of public discourse and the best way to satisfy the needs of both the private individual and the community.

Actors and groups that make up global civil society are bound together by the principle of global solidarity, which implies unity and camaraderie with victims of human rights violations of regimes in different parts of the global village, regardless of their own governments' support or lack of support for these regimes[11]. Indeed,

---

[7] Realizing Rights: The Ethical Globalization Initiative Website, http://www.eginitiative.org. (Accessed 12 October 2005).

[8] Watson, 2001, p 11.

[9] Monshipouri and Welch, 2001, p 384.

[10] Kiely, Ray. *The Clash of Civilisations. Neo-Liberalism, the Third Way and anti-Globalisation.* Brill, Leiden and Boston, 2005 p 227.

[11] Kiely, 2005 p 248.

whilst globalisation is often criticised for opening a 'participatory gap'[12], defined as the exclusion of groups and individuals from traditional policymaking processes, it is also responsible for the emergence of new types of transnational networks which have the capacity to bridge this gap. In other words, globalisation has opened up new opportunities for civil society to engage in transnational political mobilisation and construct global political strategies to campaign for human rights and good governance[13].

'Human rights' are 'human rights' in any language

Some question the viability of the concept of 'global solidarity', given the different material circumstances faced by people across the world. And when global civil society demands the recognition of 'human rights', whose definition of human rights is being promoted, given the diversity of cultures and orientations in the 'global community'?

Globalisation is not necessarily synonymous with global homogenisation, and different factors and influences will continue to sustain differences amongst societies. However, just as globalisation has helped create a sharing of information, capital, goods and services across national boundaries, the world today is also facing shared problems of insecurity caused by transnational criminal actors such as terrorists, international crime syndicates, human traffickers and people smugglers. The subordination of human values to corporate profits, as evidenced by the exploitation of poor farmers in the Third World by powerful multinational corporations, is causing serious concerns internationally. Finally, the absence of democracy and breaches of human rights in authoritarian regimes such as those in China, Iran, Burma and Syria remain despite growing international human rights awareness.

---

[12] Witte, Jan Martin, Reinicke, Wolfgang and Benner, Thorsten. *Beyond multilateralism: Global public policy networks.* International Politics and Society. (February 2000), sourced from the Internet, http://www.fes.de/IPG/ipg2_2000/artwitte.html (Accessed 14th October 2005).

[13] Adamson, Fiona. *Globalisation, Transnational Political Mobilisation, and Networks of Violence.* Cambridge Review of International Affairs. Volume 18, No.1 (April 2005) pp 32-49 at 33.

Some challenge the notion of universal human rights. One writer, David Gillies[14], contends that there are just four core rights - freedom from torture and other forms of cruel and inhuman treatment, freedom from hunger, freedom from discrimination, and freedom from arbitrary and extrajudicial killing - that apply to every human being. This short list seems to present day authors extremely narrow, and Liberal political thought promotes the belief that human values are 'the same in every community', and that 'basic human needs and responses transcend race, religion or language based culture'[15]. It is not Western or Eurocentric imperialism to maintain that the rights in international instruments like the Universal Declaration of Human Rights, the International Covenant on Civil and Political Rights and the International Covenant on Economic, Social and Cultural Rights are the entitlement of every person in the world. However, recognising that all individuals have valid claims to human rights is one thing; enforcing these rights is quite another.

Globalisation as a Human Rights Process

Globalisation as a human rights observance, advocacy and protection process is primarily based on dialogue. This dialogue is primarily based on values, and is carried out using a common language of respect and solidarity. This dialogue has also necessitated an agreement on some sharing of responsibilities for finding solutions to human rights problems between governments, international organisations, the business sector and civil society.

How is this 'dialogue' facilitated, given that a significant portion of global society does not have, or has been deprived of, a voice? The strength of globalisation as an instrument of emancipation and empowerment lies in its ability to arm the most vulnerable individuals in society with a powerful weapon - knowledge. Globalised information technology has facilitated the development of a knowledge-based civil society. Whilst old technologies like fax and fixed line telephones

---

[14] Monshipouri and Welch, 2001 cite David Gillies *Between Principle and Practice: Human Rights in North-South Relations* (1996).

[15] Watson, 2001, p 88.

continue to enable the rapid exchange of information, the Internet, email, cable and satellite television and mobile telephones have proven to be even more powerful and effective in the global dialogue on human rights.

The Internet

The Internet began as a military project which later transformed into a civilian network used by millions of people[16]. Through the Internet, it is now possible to access information from websites dedicated to human rights advocacy, observance and protection, and download and distribute voluminous information for a low cost. The search engines on the Internet are useful tools for research. The simple task of typing a keyword often reveals an abundance of sources and information on the subject selected. The websites of human rights NGOs such as Amnesty International and Human Rights Watch give access to up-to-date country information and case studies regarding the human rights situation in different parts of the world. There is also a plethora of websites devoted to lobbying and campaigning in a specific national or ethnic cause or to address specific problems. They often contain detailed, uncensored first person narratives of experiences of abuse and human rights violations that cannot be obtained elsewhere due to censorship restrictions.

In addition to providing information, the Internet has also made it possible for people to communicate and distribute information through electronic mail. Email is also a popular medium of communication for lobbying politicians and other government authorities whose contact details are publicly available on the Internet. Another form of communication via the Internet is 'chatting' in newsrooms and chatrooms, which provide the opportunity for real-time conversations between Internet users. Internet users can choose between a number of rooms categorised according to age, culture, religious beliefs or interests, and communicate with people visiting the same room. NGOs

---

[16] Public Interest Law Initiative *Durban Symposium on Public Interest Law: Workshops.* Sourced from the Internet http://www.pili.org/publications/durban/internet.html (Accessed 4th October 2005).

are known to hold meetings in newsrooms and chatrooms, not only with their own members but also with members of the public.

The Internet has for instance been instrumental in raising awareness regarding domestic abuse and honour killings in the Middle East, particularly amongst the victims themselves. The relative anonymity afforded by women's rights websites has allowed them to provide legal, social and psychological assistance to women and has provided a forum where they could engage in discussions with other victims about a subject that is traditionally taboo. In Jordan, women's groups use the Internet to coordinate their efforts with women's groups in neighbouring countries, according to Asma Khader, leading Jordanian advocate in the campaign against honour crimes[17].

Mobile Telephones

The popularity of mobile or cellular telephones in global communications is undeniable. The new advances in mobile phone technology enable the user to access the Internet, send and receive text and multimedia messages at high speed, take photographs and converse with another caller[18]. Mobile telephones are increasingly being used to disseminate news and information, as well as for supporting human rights petitions. In Africa, a news and information agency, Fahamu, launched an initiative in 2004 to rally mobile telephone users to send text messages in support of a petition for women's rights in Africa, to complement the existing online petition[19].

Television and satellite dishes

In addition to the Internet and mobile telephones, globalisation has made it possible to access news and information from a variety of different news providers, such as the Cable News Network (CNN) or

---

[17] *Women's Empowerment* The Washington Report on Middle East Affairs. (30th April 2001).

[18] Macan-Markar, Marwaan Rights-East Asia: 'Compensated dating' draws young into sex trade, Global Information Network, 27th April 2004.

[19] Choike.Org *Africa Mobile phone users rally for women's rights* (29th July 2004) http://www.choike.org/nuevo_eng/informes/2189.html (Accessed 4th October 2005).

British Broadcasting Corporation (BBC). Access to free and unrestricted information is particularly important in authoritarian and oppressive societies, where the national news channels are government-controlled. A welcome addition to the international services of the BBC is Talking Point, which allows viewers and listeners from different parts of the world to take part in live discussions on particular issues, either via the Internet or by telephone. Globalisation has indeed facilitated the creation of a global information society.

Civil society

Globalisation has been instrumental in the dissemination of information as regards the human rights violations committed in different countries in the world, and the existence of networks of human rights campaigners and supporters. Civil society organisations remain the most valuable resource for the promotion of universal human rights. Without them, the mobilisation of people, knowledge and resources for human rights observance, protection and promotion would not at all be possible.

Unlike the Internet and mobile telephones which only disseminate information, international human rights and development NGOs and transnational organisations also *educate* individuals and groups in relation to their rights and entitlements. They possess in-depth and expert knowledge of international human rights covenants and conventions, are aware of reports on the human rights performance of different governments, and participate in meetings and projects organised by global and supranational associations of governments such as the United Nations and the European Union. Their activities have helped reverse the lack of awareness about international standards amongst the general public and have motivated a growing interest in the subject. Former Secretary General Boutros Ghali affirmed that NGOs are an "indispensable part of the legitimacy" of the United Nations, and his successor, Kofi Annan, has referred to NGOs as "the conscience of humanity"[20].

---

[20] Selian, Audrey. *The World Summit on the Information Society and Civil Society*. The Information Society. Volume 20, 2004, pp. 201-215 at 206.

Globalisation as a political strategy for the achievement of human rights

Globalisation has also changed the environment in which politics operates. The demands for rights and entitlements are no longer fought exclusively by national actors within the territorial jurisdiction of the sovereign state. Rather, the dialogue on human rights is now being conducted both upwards at the supranational, international and global levels, and downwards, at the level of the individual and the local, also known as 'glocalisation'[21]. Globalisation and the liberalisation of access to knowledge have inevitably fostered the rise of a new understanding of the 'common language of humanity'[22]. In the post Cold War era therefore, states are forced to make difficult ethical, legal and political choices, as they are held to higher moral standards.

As a political strategy for the achievement of human rights, globalisation comes in the form of political mobilisation. This process involves political resources such as information and manpower being made accessible to non-state actors in the form of a human rights-driven civil society. Those non-state actors then engage in a political dialogue with established institutions of political power for the protection and promotion of human rights.

Human Rights Monitoring

Although many states have ratified human rights instruments, ratification does not automatically mean compliance. Transnational human rights networks such as NGOs are engaged in the monitoring of the conduct of states in regard to either their recognition or violation of the human rights of their citizens. They also conduct field visits to countries and sites of human rights violations, gather data, conduct interviews and produce reports containing an evaluation of the state's treatment of its citizens and respect for international human rights instruments. They exert pressure on states to improve their human rights

---

[21] Swyngedouw, Erik. *Globalisation or Glocalisation? Networks, Territories and Rescaling.* Cambridge Review of International Affairs. Volume 17, No.1 (April 2004) pp 25-48.

[22] Monshipouri and Welch, 2001 p 372.

situation and implement necessary reforms by distributing their reports to other governments, international organisations and experts.

Campaigning

The strength of human rights advocates, supporters and leaders lies in their ability to be seen and heard. Campaigning implies soliciting support for a particular cause, and 'anti-campaigning'[23] implies an active resistance to forces that contribute to the violation of human rights, such as the 'anti-war', 'anti-debt', and 'anti-sweatshop' campaigns which featured prominently in the 1999 WTO protests in Seattle. Transnational human rights groups have at their disposal - due to globalisation - a number of different media to get their message across. Due to their expertise and perceived moral authority, they are able not only to influence the way people think, but also encourage the public to participate in their activities and make a monetary donation to their cause.

The Pinochet case demonstrates the extension of human rights standards, albeit largely European, to another region, Latin America, where culture and tradition called for a substantial deference to state power and a political deference paid to leaders drawn from the armed forces. The case has set new precedents against the impunity of dictators and war criminals, and transnational human rights networks and NGOs played an important and active role in the process[24].

Direct participation or intervention

Due to their expertise and knowledge, the participation of transnational human rights groups and NGOs in global summits and conferences has been highly sought after. Through this, they are able to engage in political dialogue with governments, international and global actors and organisations in areas they have a vast knowledge of. For example, the UN agency responsible for the protection of children, UNICEF, actively engages the support and expertise of human rights organisations in its

---

[23] Kiely, 2005 p 226.

[24] Human Rights Watch *The Pinochet Precedent,* sourced from the Internet, http://www.hrw.org/campaigns/chile98/precedent.htm (Accessed 4th October 2005).

activities. The Earth Summit was also considered to be a 'defining moment' for civil society participation, when they were awarded consultative status with ECOSOC in the Commission on Sustainable Development[25].

Globalisation and the Nation State

"I am convinced that despite the many changes that globalisation has wrought the primary responsibility for protecting human rights remains with national governments"[26].

It is clear that globalisation is increasingly becoming an effective instrument in allowing individuals, groups and civil society to actively engage in the dialogue on human rights across national boundaries. However, there exists, between the nation state and the international arena, a 'supranational tier' in the form most obviously of the European Union. The institutions of the EU, particularly the European Parliament, are a perfect example of the change in environment in which formal politics and the human rights dialogue operates. The lobbying of civil society and human rights groups assisted the fulfilment of demands by MEPs that the protection of citizens' rights be incorporated into the EU treaties[27].

What does this mean for the nation state? In a globalising world, the nation state would need to recognise the multiplicity of actors and the new arenas in which the dialogue on human rights is being deliberated. However, taking state sovereignty for granted in discussions of human rights would underestimate 'the tragic ironies inherent in the

---

[25] Selian, 2004 at 211.

[26] Robinson, Mary *'Towards an Ethnical Globalisation: Meeting the challenges of an interconnected and divided world'.* The International Council on Human Rights Policy 'Wilson's Cat' lecture, University of Geneva, Switzerland, 26th November 2003. Transcript of speech sourced from http://www.eginitiative.org (Accessed 4th October 2005).

[27] Gavin, Brigid. *The European Union and Globalisation. Towards Global Democratic Governance,* Edward Elgar Publishing Limited, 2001, pp 15-16.

contemporary system of national enforcement' of these rights[28]. Mary Robinson, former Irish President and UN Human Rights Commissioner and now Executive Director of *'Realizing Rights: The Ethical Globalisation Initiative'*, believes that despite the changes brought about by globalisation, the responsibility for protecting human rights remains with national governments, and that the best long term strategy for securing the rights and interests of the people is to build the capacities of national governments.

However, the assertion that sovereignty is 'sacrosanct' is no longer tenable. Whilst human rights obligations can only be fulfilled with the approval and consent of the state, the dialogue on human rights is no longer conducted exclusively within the confines of the state. Thanks to globalisation, all actors, whether individual, group, private or public, vulnerable or powerful, now have a voice in the dialogue.

Globalisation, human rights advocacy and the future

"...there is no alternative to globalisation. It is happening whether we want it or not. ... in reality the integration of markets has progressed so far that such action would have immediate negative effects on the economy. ... Furthermore, technological progress, especially in the fields of information and communication, is one of the key driving forces of economic globalisation and is irreversible. Therefore, fighting against globalisation is, to put it in economic terms, a waste of resources" [29].

Critics of globalisation as an instrument of human rights advocacy argue that it is not an effective tool for the empowerment of vulnerable people as it is currently not yet available to those who need it most, it mainly caters for the Western audience, and it puts at risk the lives of already vulnerable people. Indeed, cyber dissidents Yang Zili from China, Mojtaba Saminebad from Iran and Zouhair Yahyaoui from Tunisia - all nominees for the 2005 Sakharov Prize - were all put in prison for their use of the Internet and for publishing details of their country's

---

[28] Monshipouri and Welch, 2001 pp 375 - 376.

[29] Hoyer, Werner *Globalisation, Social Market Economies and Development* in Watson, 2001, p. 41.

authoritarian practices. Poverty and lack of education have also deprived ethnic minorities and women of access to the Internet and other modern forms of communication. It has also been widely acknowledged that most websites and materials on human rights are available only in the English language.

But this is a reason to keep on battling for the advantages of globalisation in the promotion of human rights to be spread more widely! While acknowledging that the globalisation balance sheet in economic, social and environmental areas is mixed, the 'human rights' account has a healthy surplus. We should continue to take ever more advantage of the benefits that it brings and celebrate the sense of global solidarity which it has created, without which the sense of 'global humanity', pivotal in the promotion of borderless, universal human rights, would not have come into being.

Jules Maaten MEP

"What is prudence in the conduct of every family can scarce be folly in that of a great kingdom. If a foreign country can supply us with a commodity cheaper than we ourselves can make it, better buy it off them with some part of the produce of our own industry, employed in a way in which we have some advantage."[1]

It is hard to state the case for globalisation more clearly. But equally, avid believers in international economic integration cannot avoid the question of whether it works for everybody and for whom it works best. After all, if one believes in globalisation, is that because of a nostalgic loyalty to Adam Smith, or because more pragmatically it actually solves some of the problems that we face in the world?

There are many reasons why the theoretical approach is not to be favoured. In today's society, with increasingly critical citizens who believe in policies that work in practice not in theory, we have to be able to demonstrate - not merely explain - that globalisation is an opportunity, not a threat. Moreover, globalisation is only worth supporting if it works, not because of some love affair with liberal dogma. For example, economic inequality is not somehow justified as a sad necessity sanctified by the market, as Martin Wolf convincingly writes[2]. The market can solve many problems, but by no means all and a strong state is needed to organise matters.

In this essay I shall argue that international economic integration, whether on a global or European scale, has allowed policy makers to deny some of their responsibilities thus contributing to a general dissatisfaction with politics among the greater public. However, on the contrary international economic integration calls for an active role of the state because globalisation and certain social policies go hand in hand. I shall also argue that democracy, far from being under threat from globalisation, is the answer to some of the problems caused by a

---

[1] Smith, A., *The Wealth of Nations*, (1776).

[2] Wolf, M., *Why Globalisation Works* (Yale, 2004).

malfunctioning of international economic integration. Finally I shall examine the proposition that international economic integration can only be considered a success if citizens and consumers benefit from it, and that they will only do so if both politics and the economy are subjected to a system of proper checks and balances.

Globalisation is not only about the denationalisation of markets and the creation of a global economy. The level of democratisation of the world affects how well a liberal economy functions.

Globalisation is the most effective force known to mankind for reducing poverty in the third world. On the whole it has led to a stronger world economy, yet it has bypassed some of the poorest countries. It need not be so. It is not their poverty that makes these countries unsuitable to international economic integration. The poorest countries are often states where fundamental tasks such as the providing security of property and establishing the rule of law are left undone. What can be done about these states? Ideally Western liberal democracies are taken as an example by the rest of the world. The recent foreign policy of the United States has been somewhat inspired by the wish to spread liberal democracy in the world. George Bush seems to have made it his primary mission to free the world from tyranny and terror and to install democratic regimes wherever possible. He has found a soul mate in Natan Sharansky, whose book *The Case for Democracy: The Power of Freedom to Overcome Tyranny and Terror*[3] can be summarised as a three-fold message. First, that 'realpolitik' is bankrupt. He argues that the US cannot continue to support tyrannical regimes because those regimes try to buy stability at home by exporting hatred abroad. Secondly, Sharansky states that democracy is the best insurance against aggression and finally he concludes that the world really is divided between good and evil. This is what we could call the Bush-Sharansky 'freedom doctrine', although it is debatable how seriously and consistently the Bush administration puts the doctrine into practice. But does the European Union have any greater credibility?

---

[3] Sharansky, N. *The Case for Democracy: The Power of Freedom to Overcome Tyranny and Terror* (2004).

To date, the European Union has not had much in the way of foreign policy, let alone foreign policy doctrine. However, it is high time that the EU starts playing an active role in the advocacy of liberal democracy outside its own borders. In the proposed Constitutional Treaty a basis for the development of proper and consistent EU foreign policy was laid down in the form of an EU Foreign Affairs Minister. Although it is unlikely that this Minister will be put in place any time soon, that should not prevent Europe from beginning to model her own 'freedom doctrine'. The question is of course along what lines this doctrine should be shaped. Europe tends to be rather critical when it comes to the US, and particularly so of the current US foreign policy. However the first two elements of the Bush-Sharansky doctrine - the end of realpolitik and the idea that democracy is the best insurance against aggression - deserve to play an important role in future European foreign policy.

Globalisation is often perceived as the spread of Western liberal economic and democratic standards through the world. Liberal globalisation could be described as the extension of the three freedoms espoused by John Stuart Mill (economic, personal and civic freedom) over a global scale, even if the spread of economic liberalism and democracy do not always go hand in hand.

Who champions the cause of globalisation? Is it global companies? Is it rich countries? Governments of poor nations? For a liberal the champions can only be citizens and consumers, both in rich and poor nations. The yardstick for measuring whether globalisation works is whether they are any better off.

The recipe is increased economic integration, rather than fragmentation. Wolf argues that the European Union as a regional system of jurisdictional integration served as an extraordinarily successful machine for generating economic catch-up among previously poorer members, from Italy in the 1950s and 1960s to Ireland in the 1990s. Of course economic integration, while good, is by itself not sufficient. A variety of steps need to be taken to enlarge the benefits flowing to the poor, as Jagdish Bhagwati notes[4].

---

[4] Bhagwati, J., *In Defense of Globalization* (Oxford, 2004).

Economic integration limits what governments, particularly oppressive ones, can do. Without doubt, oppression is more difficult with open borders. People can leave and take their savings with them. Global markets are thus an ally of human rights and of democracy.

If we look at the success of global internet firms, such as Yahoo!, Google, Amazon and eBay, we see that they survive because of their agility and because they listen carefully to their consumers. That is economic democracy. And with economics as well as news, information and debate being globalised by the internet with its relatively low barriers, it is inconceivable that these consumers, the internet's true sovereigns, will only formulate their views on their purchases, and not on everything else that matters to their lives.

In recent years Western liberal democracy has taken quite a few blows. Not only from the outside - by terrorist attacks and other external threats to our basic liberties - but also from the inside. The question posed by these developments is whether Western democracies can still be perceived as role models and as initiators of liberal globalisation.

The fundamental elements of liberal democracy - free and fair elections, the rule of law, separation of powers and the protection of basic liberties of speech, assembly, religion and property are at the heart of most Western societies. Until now globalisation, i.e. the process of denationalisation of markets, politics and legal systems and the rise of the so-called global economy has more or less taken place along the lines and the principles of Western liberal democracy. When listening to anti-globalists you will find that their arguments turn mainly against the global spread of capitalism or economic liberalism. They tend to forget that liberalism is not only about money and markets. In this light it is useful to look at a concept which American publicist and editor of *Newsweek International,* Fareed Zakaria, calls constitutional liberalism. According to Zakaria constitutional liberalism seeks to protect an individual's autonomy and dignity against coercion (by the state, the church or society). He distinguishes two elements in his concept, a liberal element which emphasises individual liberty, and a constitutional element which focuses on the rule of law. Zakaria argues that liberalism, both in its political and in its economic sense, may have coincided with the rise of democracy, but it has never been unambiguously linked to its practice[5].

Liberalism, democracy and globalisation are connected but it does not follow that they always necessarily or automatically go hand in hand.

A further example of the relationship of these three elements is that of central Europe. Countries such as Poland, Hungary, and the Czech Republic established regimes that protected individual rights, including those of property and contract, and that created a framework of law and administration, capitalism and economic growth followed almost automatically. As Alan Greenspan put it, "The guiding mechanism of a free market economy . . . is a bill of rights, enforced by an impartial judiciary.[6]"

Big budget deficits, higher taxes, more public ownership of industry are anathema to the majority of any electorate. They elect political parties who favour policies that open up their society, even if that means that their politicians say that they then have less scope to take their own decisions on economic and other matters (what Thomas Friedman of the *New York Times* calls the 'Golden Straitjacket', when "the economy grows and the politics shrink")[7]. Most voters support straitjacket policies, but not, it seems, with much enthusiasm. There is a recurring sense of bowing down to forces more powerful than liberal democracy - the markets, the multinationals, the WTO and the IMF. This disenchantment is in itself a kind of democratic failure. In the same way that EU Member States' government ministers blame the European Union for all evils, politicians also play a part in perpetuating the myth that globalisation gives them a lesser say in the running of society. This

---

[5] Zakaria, F., *The Rise of Illiberal Democracy*
www.fareedzakaria.com/articles/other/democracy.html (accessed 15th November 2005).

[6] Speech to Woodrow Wilson Award Dinner, New York, 10th June 1997,
www.federalreserve.gov/boarddocs/speeches/1997/19970610.htm, accessed 15th November 2005.

[7] Friedman, T., *The Lexus and the Olive Tree* (New York, 1999).

denial of responsibility, the pretence that policies are dictated by global markets rather than by elected governments and the refusal to consider alternatives are all profoundly corrosive to democracy.

In different parts and on various levels of the Western world, democracy has suffered a crisis of legitimacy. This is highlighted by the attempts of the US and EU to spread liberal and constitutional democracy worldwide. Tension between democracy and liberalism has become evident over the last few years in the United States. Few Americans still believe in the power of their elected politicians, something which is proven by the decreased turn out at elections (only 60% at the last Presidential elections[8]). The American citizen tends to have more faith in the power of lobbyists, NGO's, think tanks, the press and private enterprises than in the government.

On the other side of the Atlantic Ocean, the recent rejection of the European Constitution by the French and Dutch citizens draws an even darker picture. The Treaty that was intended to increase citizens' influence over the European decision-making process and that was to make the first steps towards reducing the famous democratic deficit of the European Union was vigorously rejected by those citizens it aimed to involve more in the European democratic process. On a European level the democratic deficit can only be solved if trust in both European and national politicians is restored.

The proposed EU Constitutional Treaty, took a real, albeit small, step towards more democratic and transparent institutions. But, at the same time, the Treaty fell short in creating a true European political arena which could be held accountable by every European. Therefore the EU should now consider a more radical approach. The citizens of Europe directly electing the President of the European Commission, or introducing a European corrective referendum, or enabling national parliaments to reject a European law on subsidiarity grounds are just a few of the many possibilities which might restore checks and balances to European democracy.

---

[8] www.guardian.co.uk/uselections2004/0,13918,1047353,00.html. (accessed 14th November 2005).

The discontent with the European Constitution does not only find its source in discontent about European policy and policy-making. A large part of it is inspired by a general aversion against politicians.

Society is under pressure and freedom no longer goes without saying. Trust, the cement of any society, is diminishing. There is a variety of reasons for this phenomenon: a growing level of crime, terrorism, rule-mania and tax pressure, economic stagnation, slumbering ethnic tension and failing education all leading to dissatisfaction, mistrust and confusion. The key to preserving freedom is a revaluation of the state. The main political problem of our time is the mistrust of the state by the citizens. Liberals want to renew this trust by making it clear that the citizens are in charge.

In the view of Liberals, international economic integration results when technology allows people to pursue their own goals and they are given the liberty to do so. A liberal outlook is consistent with support for a wide range of government interventions; indeed a liberal outlook demands many such interventions. The point of a liberal market economy is, after all, that it civilises the quest for profit, turning it into an engine of social progress. Under a market system, economic interaction is voluntary. There is no reason to fear that economic integration threatens national identities, except in so far as individual freedom threatens them.

Zakaria advocates a renewed trust in our elected politicians, not through more democracy but through less of it. He sees the need for responsible people who dare to take the lead without being influenced by the emotional reactions of the public in the short term.

Whatever the merits of this philosophy, Europe should take a lead in exporting her constitutional democracy to the rest of the world and not leave this important mission to the US alone. However, since the EU and some of her Member States are going through what could be termed a democratic identity crisis, one might wonder if Western liberal democracy should not be redefined altogether.

A different approach is needed, for the sake of both democracy and globalisation. Even the most elementary account of democracy recognises the need for checks and balances. This is true for political democracy (where the will of the people does not always prevail, but, for example, minorities have special rights, endangered species are protected, human rights are upheld, the constitution goes before the will of the majority of the day, and so on) and equally as much for economic democracy. The global flow of information, a by-product of the integration of markets, works to the same effect. Through informing citizens about alternatives, they are made more demanding. And a country's position in a globalising world is made stronger, not weaker, by increasing public spending on education and health, which raises productivity by producing a healthier and more contented workforce with better labour relations and greater labour mobility. Therefore letting the citizen and the consumer come first benefits all.

Philippe Morillon MEP

The victory of the rather disparate 'no' camp in the French referendum on the ratification of the Constitutional Treaty marks the end of a process that began at the last presidential election in France. It bears witness to a total lack of trust in the country's political leaders and reminds us of a phenomenon that arose fifty years ago with the short-lived success of the populist movement Poujadism, inspired by a single objective: the destruction of the institutions of the moment.

It may be deplorable but in the face of globalisation the vast majority of our contemporaries do not react in the spirit of 'citizens of the world'. On the contrary, the main trend seems to be not self-containment but assertion of identity, and nationalist, micro-nationalist and regionalist movements have never been more vigorous and sometimes, unfortunately, more violent.

It is as if people had had an attack of vertigo at the prospect of globalisation and had reacted by feeling the need to reaffirm their roots in the land where they were born and the culture in which they were raised.

Bosnia: The need for identity

As commander of the United Nations Protection Force in Bosnia-Herzegovina thirteen years ago, I was confronted on the ground by this phenomenon as I met representatives of the Serbian, Croatian and Muslim communities who had been fighting each other during the five years of violence, heroism and destruction prior to December 1995, when the Dayton agreement was signed, thus creating a narrow opening for a fragile peace, which still today has not been sufficient for a return to true cohabitation.

Many in the West thought that this crisis had been deliberately provoked by partisans of a 'Greater Serbia' or 'Greater Croatia' who wanted to profit from the break-up of the Communist regime to establish their dominance over all or part of the unfortunate province. I maintain that although some of the politicians on every side and every ethnic group were undeniably responsible for initiating the crisis, the vast majority of the people themselves wanted to go on living in peace and enjoying the richness and diversity of their cultures.

At the beginning of 1992 the capital, Sarajevo, was a model of a cosmopolitan city where there were no ghettos, and the bells of the Croatian Catholic cathedral rang out as loud as those of the Serbian Orthodox churches and the calls of the Muslim muezzins. It was a city where Serbs, Croats and Muslims lived in perfect understanding in the same buildings, mostly quite unaware of who was Serb, Croat or Muslim among them.

It was the fear of other, different, people, a disease deliberately propagated by awakening memories of past atrocities, which threw these communities against each other in an infernal spiral of blood and violence.

The Serbs, for example, who at that time gathered in the hills around Sarajevo, did not go there because they wanted to dominate Bosnia, but because some of their leaders had told them that if they did not go, their wives would be forced to wear the Islamic veil.

It was the same for the Croats who along the length of the Neretva valley clashed mercilessly with their Muslim neighbours, who in Sarajevo and Mostar and over the whole country had no other option but to leave their towns and villages as victims of the ethnic cleansing policy, or to barricade themselves in and drive out those who were not of the same faith.

In the middle of all this madness, where it was my job to establish the conditions for peace, I understood what could be the role of the international community and in particular the European Union. This role was, and remains today, by its very existence and presence to calm the fear of being overrun, the fear of being wiped out, a fear which crops up regularly and disastrously in the history of this country every time an external power ceases to ensure that balance is maintained.

Through history this was the role of the Ottoman Empire, the Austro-Hungarian Empire, and Tito, who built his power on a reconciliation pact, and I repeat, today it is the role of Europe.

When I recently met Croatian and Muslim inhabitants of Mostar, which remains the only major multiethnic Bosnian city, they confirmed to me that the only thing that brought them together was their feeling of certainty that they are European.

This underlies my conviction that the way we should continue to build the European Union is by making sure that it preserves identities.

Europe - what is it for?

We shall never build the United States of Europe in the image of the United States of America which, since the end of the War of Independence, is the fruit of a monoculture. Europe is rich in its diversity and the Alliance of Liberals and Democrats for Europe are well aware that the aim of European integration must be to preserve this wealth by ensuring that the different cultures which have blossomed on this continent throughout its history are maintained.

In the extreme conditions of the break-up of the Federal Republic of Yugoslavia, we saw that people felt so strongly about maintaining these diversities that they attacked each other in the most barbaric conflicts.

This is what happened in the last century on the opposite banks of the Rhine, until the genius of Europe's founding fathers brought Franco-German reconciliation, unimaginable for the men and women of my parents' generation.

It was in the acceptance of mutual dependency that the fear which reigned for generations between two peoples was conquered, peoples who now wonder how there could have been such a degree of hatred between them in the past. This is the model on which the European Union was built, but I am always struck by seeing how much it has been able to achieve with patience and understanding, enabling each of its Member States not to lose any part of their identity.

Today, following the failures of the French and Dutch referenda, we must keep hold of this idea so that we can relaunch the process of European integration by implementing the institutional reforms that are needed.

We are Europeans because we are patriots. In the face of galloping globalisation where we can see the risk of losing our soul, we need the EU, covering a continent which shares the same values but in which each state, each region, and each province in some cases is determined to preserve its roots.

This is why I do not share the opinion of those who, even within our own political group, advocate abandoning our national languages and adopting instead a universal language which could only be a bastardised form of English which each one of us would mangle at will.

I have not forgotten the emotion felt by our friends from the East at being able to speak in their own languages in the European Parliament when they finally joined last year. Latvians, Estonians, Lithuanians, Poles, Czechs, Slovaks, Hungarians and Slovenes, after decades of humiliating restriction, gave us the impression that they were breathing large gulps of hope and even pure happiness. And this happiness was, I am sure, shared by our Maltese and Cypriot friends who joined at same time, and by those who were lucky enough to take part in the event.

The Europe which welcomed them then was the fruit of a miraculous balance where each one, whether 'small' or 'large', was able to develop while remaining true to theirselves. It is that balance which we in the ALDE hope and intend to preserve.

We must ask how we can achieve this despite the failure of the consultations in France and the Netherlands on the adoption of the Constitution

In 1956, during the last parliamentary elections of the Fourth Republic, many voters were appalled by the political and financial scandals marking the end of the Indochina War and weary of the inability of successive governments to push through the necessary reforms. They responded *en masse* to the call of an unknown leader, Pierre Poujade, the 'stationer of Saint Céré', and founder and leader of the Union de défense des commerçants et artisans, whose sole aim during the campaign was to 'oust the incumbents'. Two years later, admittedly with the help of the Algerian crisis, came the arrival of the Fifth Republic and the adoption of the new, made-to-measure, or perhaps it would be more accurate to say made-to-excess, constitution of General de Gaulle.

The crisis occurring in France today is to my mind exactly like the one I have just mentioned. If the Constitutional Treaty had had to be ratified solely by members of the national assembly in Versailles, it would have received an overwhelming majority of votes. Its rejection by the French nation should not cause us to consider rewriting the European Constitution but rather to consider changing our national institutions. We need to radically reform our regime, which has now been rejected by our fellow citizens.

Without oversimplifying, the regime over the last twenty-five years since President François Mitterrand came to power has consisted of the rapid alternation of two apparently opposing factions, in and out of power, representing the right and the left of the political spectrum. At a time when major divisions such as the split over Europe are no longer between left and right but lie within each of these political families, traditional rivalries have become increasingly artificial and French voters have begun to feel this quite consciously. Thus we can explain the gradual rejection of a system based on the UK model that produces comfortable parliamentary majorities by means of elections designed to achieve this. The Union pour la Démocratie Française (UDF) - and its chairman, François Bayrou - was well aware of this during the last campaign in 2002 for the election of the French President. It had urged the opening of a third way that would allow government from the centre and unite two out of three French voters on the objectives of this government. Sadly for France and now for Europe, too, not enough attention was paid to him.

On 21st April we received the shock of the first round results in which the socialist candidate was eliminated and a candidate from the extreme right went through to the second round. The message should have been clear. It marked the exasperation of the electorate with the increasingly apparent inability of the establishment to put forward and implement the reforms needed to deal with the crisis. Rightly or wrongly, those within this establishment were increasingly seen as enjoying guaranteed incomes and positions in a system where they merely had to wait periodically in the temporary comfort of opposition for the dish of power to be served up to them again.

The system had gradually been perverted to the point that this alternation was occurring more and more frequently, complicated more often than not by the phenomenon of 'cohabitation' between a President and a Prime Minister of opposing camps. Under these circumstances and regardless of the courage and personal qualities of the leaders, how can we benefit from the continuity and consistency required for the exercise of power?

Unable to find an answer to this question, French citizens used their votes on 21st April simply to say 'enough is enough'. Grassroots France could not have been much more explicit. Sadly it was not heard by those at the top. Instead of working all out to mend the fault line that had appeared in public opinion, Jacques Chirac and his advisors did everything they could to increase it by setting up the Union pour la Majorité Présidentielle. Forgetting that they could only count on a minority of votes from their fellow citizens, within the framework of these institutions they conceived and established an anti-democratic system concentrating total power in the hands of its supporters.

At each vote held since - the recent regional and European elections and now the European referendum - the French have continued to reject this option. Perhaps it's not too late to listen.

Among the possible solutions for dealing with what François Bayrou was right to call a very serious crisis, I believe we can draw inspiration from the experiment conducted over a year ago within the European Parliament.

On the return to Parliament at the start of the current term, after lengthy preliminary discussions, the decision was made to set up the Alliance of Liberals and Democrats for Europe, enabling the constitution of a group of around a hundred MEPs at the centre of the parliamentary chamber, chaired by Graham Watson. Practically all the major votes that have taken place in plenary since then have followed our recommendations. It has thus been demonstrated that a centre group such as ours can have a determining influence on the decisions of an assembly shared between a right wing in the form of the European People's Party and a left wing consisting mainly of the Party of European Socialists.

To reconcile public opinion with a political class in which it lacks confidence, we need to break down the increasingly artificial and therefore sterile divisions between left and right and give power to the centre.

But what will government from the centre set out to achieve? Within the UDF, the party in France most involved in pursuing and completing the construction of Europe, we spent a long time reflecting on this prior to the distressing referendum failure - particularly when we sealed the alliance within the European Parliament uniting us with our liberal friends.

I think we share with them the conviction that the only solution to globalisation is to strengthen the European Union so that each of its Member States is able to retain its own identity.

Having been caught up in the bloody drama that unfolded in the Balkans more than ten years ago, I'm better placed than many to know that humans carry deep within them the often unconscious desire to keep their roots in the soil on which they were born and in the culture in which they were raised. I am convinced that this need only increases as globalisation intensifies. We may not like it, but very few of our contemporaries actually want to be global citizens. On the contrary, in a reaction to the way the world is changing, as I said before, most of them feel the need to hold on to their heritage, which explains the increasing attraction of regionalism. The French example of the aspirations of the

Corsicans and Basques, and the British example of the Scots and Welsh illustrate, if it were necessary, the need for 21st century man to affirm his identity.

We must do all we can to make Europe a political and economic power capable not of competing with the United States but of continuing to coexist in alliance with it in order to take its place in the concert of nation-continents developing today with the emergence of China and India.

As we build this power, let us set ourselves the goal of preserving the richness of our continent by allowing all of its component parts to continue to exist unchanged within it.

As we set out these facts, it becomes apparent that this goal cannot be claimed and appropriated by either right or left. The campaign for the French referendum was a clear demonstration of how divisions on this issue run right down the middle of each of the two political families.

Graham Watson is right: the future of Europe lies in the centre. Let's build it with him.

Bill Newton Dunn MEP

Internationally-organised crime is huge, and growing. If it were a country, it would be the fourth largest economy in the world.

The public, right across Europe, knows very little about the vast scale of organised crime. Local police forces in each EU Member State are supervised democratically so that the public is aware of successes and failures against local criminals. But there is no democratic oversight, or clear picture, or unified control of international crime-fighting at European level.

Local crime is fuelled by international crime. The Home Office in London estimates that each kilo of heroin sold on British streets causes over two hundred street muggings or house-burglaries. Yet they allocate almost all of their policing assets to fighting local criminals rather than large-scale international crime.

Who are these international criminal gangs? They are based mainly outside the EU in places where law enforcement is weak, employment is weak, and opportunities for corruption are strong - such as Russia, Eastern Europe & the Balkans, central Asia, China, Nigeria, Columbia and Brazil. Anywhere where there are clever people without opportunities for legitimate work. They target where the money is, which is inside the EU and the USA.

Their principal activities are:
  a. Drugs - importing heroin from Afghanistan, cocaine from Columbia, and also exporting ecstasy from Europe to the rest of the world.
  b. Smuggling counterfeit goods which are cheaply made and of low quality - such as CDs and DVDs, imitation jeans, perfumes, but also fake condoms, aircraft parts, car brakes, medicines and anti-bird flu capsules, even extending to fake baby foods, and much more. These imitations undermine honest EU workers' jobs, and oblige taxpayers to pay extra taxes to compensate for what is lost when the fakes are sold tax-free.

c. Identity theft, mainly on the internet, when gullible Europeans are persuaded to reveal their bank details, or their social security numbers, and so enable the internet thieves to steal their money.
d. Trafficking into the EU - of women for prostitution, children for paedophilia, and illegal immigrants.
e. Currency counterfeiting.
f. Violent theft of luxury cars for sale in Eastern Europe.
g. Smuggling of arms, cigarettes, alcohol, and other goods which are highly taxed in some areas of Europe, but taxed much lower in others.
h. Outlaw motorcycle groups.
i. Money laundering in order to conceal the criminal origins of money - such as the Mafia buying banks in Latvia prior to EU enlargement, and the IRA seeking to buy a Bulgarian bank before Bulgaria joins the EU.

Some terrorists finance their political activities by using organised crime. For example, the Madrid bombers sold fake CDs and DVDs to help finance their activities.

How is the European Union fighting the organised criminal gangs? The answer is that Europe's fight is probably very inadequate, but we are not being told so we do not know. The Member States do not know either because there are no standard statistics across the EU to reveal the overall extent of organised crime. Nobody knows the overall picture.

In the EU, our internal borders are open. For businessmen and individual travellers this is a huge advantage. It is for criminals too. But Europe's law enforcement agencies are all national, their officers cannot cross frontiers, and their efforts are therefore limited.

The EU has EuroPol. It is our intelligence-coordinating centre at The Hague in the Netherlands. However its officers do not have power of arrest, nor does EuroPol have power to compel any national agency to take action. It was left leaderless by the bickering Council of Ministers for over a year in 2004-5. EuroPol is an EU agency but its budget is inter-governmental, so EU citizens have no control or even insight over its spending and resources.

There is also InterPol, located at Lyon in France. This is a policemen's club entirely financed by contributions from police forces around the world. It has no officers who can make arrests. The relationship between EuroPol and InterPol is ill-defined and overlapping. Each has assets which cannot be shared with the other agency because national governments have rules which impede cooperation.

The EU has an even more serious problem. It is 'lack of trust'. Just as the Americans discovered after '9/11' that the CIA and the FBI were not cooperating but were behaving as rivals, so the same phenomenon exists in Europe but on a greater scale.

Inside Member States there is a lack of trust between neighbouring local police forces. Information is power. The owners of information are reluctant to share it. If you reveal information, it has to be authenticated by revealing what your secret source is.

Across EU internal borders, the lack of trust is much greater. What little cross-border police cooperation there is is done on the basis of personal contacts. There is no EU centre where the contact numbers and names for police in all 25 Member States can be quickly obtained. The EU Directive to enable Joint Investigation Teams has still not come into effect because not all Member States have ratified it into their own law. The protocols which would strengthen EuroPol have still not been ratified by all EU Member States and therefore have not come into effect.

Why do national leaders, who must be aware of the scale of internationally-organised crime, and who control national police forces, do so little to fight international crime? Is it because they prefer to win national elections to keep themselves in power, not European elections? They keep their police resources for combating crimes within their own state, even though international crime fuels local crimes. They win few votes from their public for diverting scarce police resources for fighting international crime because the public does not know the extent of organised international crime.

Europe's voters need to be told the true picture - of the surprising extent and great sophistication of organised criminal gangs, and of the failure of EU Member States to agree on action and powers at the EU level. Perhaps only the European Parliament can press for the needed transparency, for an end to national bickering, and for action at EU level before it is too late.

The solution, logically, is to create a European police force - which can fight the international gangs on equal terms. But it is doubtful whether the political will to do this exists in the 25 national EU capitals. Perhaps a few brave capitals should take the lead. If they formed an international force, the reluctant countries might join later when they see its success.

Baroness Nicholson of Winterbourne MEP

When I was asked to write this chapter on 'liberal democracy and globalisation' I realised that the ideal subject would be international adoptions. On the one hand international adoptions have been 'liberalised' (in a broad economic sense) since the fall of the Iron Curtain in the early 1990s; on the other hand it has become a globalised industry. In this chapter I will present a short history of international adoptions and outline my own involvement in the issue.

First of all, I should say something about my own background as this helps to explain my own motivation and drive. Before entering politics I had gained valuable experience in children's issues at Save the Children, Dr. Barnardo's National Children's Homes, Foster Parents Plan (USA) and the World Association of Girl Guides and Girl Scouts (WAGGGS). This gave me a valuable overview of the kind of problems that children face all over the world, as well as the kind of solutions that organisations and individuals look for in trying to help children in need.

While a Member of the European Parliament I was appointed to be Special Envoy for Health, Peace and Development for the World Health Organisation. I must say that this experience has enlarged my vision and focus on primary health care, an issue which includes pre and post natal child health, midwifery and the whole subject of family-based care.

All this was an excellent grounding for my first foray into Romania, in 1990, where I got involved in helping at the biggest and worst child care institution on the outskirts of Bucharest. I immediately set up the Parliamentary Appeal for Romanian Children in 1990, with colleagues from the Labour and Conservative parties (strangely enough, the Liberals were not interested back then). In 1999 the European Parliament asked me to become the Rapporteur for Romania and I naturally placed child and health issues - for all of Romania's 6.5 million children - at the top of my agenda.

What has always driven me is to try and protect children, often the most vulnerable members of a society; and when that society is weak, when its legal system is corrupt, when its public services are dysfunctional, the children are the first to suffer. I have dedicated much of my professional life to helping find the most effective policies for those children, and I am proud to be associated with Romania which is a country which has gone from having the worst child protection systems in Europe to having one of the best.

International adoption is often presented as a solution to the problems faced by children in poor countries around the world: a middle class family in the West wants to adopt a child from a poor country, often from a grim institution, and in public relations terms it often comes across as a good solution, often the only solution. One can see this phenomenon most clearly in the USA, where adoption agencies are self-regulating - in other words they can be both unscrupulous and legal.

The media tends to distort the picture when it comes to international adoptions. What is just an ordinary story of one family trying to adopt a child from another country gets transformed into a grand struggle against post-communist bureaucracy; the family are often presented as heroes and their visits to that country are described as 'mercy missions' as if their main purpose is to help develop social services rather than adopt a child. The context of these articles is that the country in question is presented in turmoil, with grim child care institutions, its people unable to look after their own children and young mothers abandon babies continually. The only solution put forward is international adoptions - whereas this should only be a possible last resort, when all other means of caring for the child in his or her country of origin have been tried and failed (viz. article 22b, United Nations Convention on the Rights of the Child - UNCRC).

This is how the public relations experts who are hired by the adoption agencies manage to spin the story - no longer is it an ordinary family trying to adopt; it has become an epic struggle between the forces of good and evil. The fact that international adoptions is often not good for the child in question, and experience shows that it has a corrupting effect in the source country, and it opens the door to the worst forms of criminal opportunity, is rarely mentioned.

I have seen this phenomenon play itself out over the last fifteen years in Romania. If one looks at the history of international adoptions from Romania you can see how it has evolved over the years; from a free-for-all in the early 1990s to an unregulated free market for children between 1997 - 2001, when children were exchanged as commodities by a fiendishly simple 'points for cash' system, where an NGO would earn x number of points and would be able to exchange these for y number of children. The international adoption business has been banned in Romania since 2001 and the new legislation, based on child rights, came into effect in 2005 (under which international adoption is only allowed for members of the extended family).

As I said above, Romania has gone from having a barbaric child care system under the Communists to having some of the best legislation in Europe. In Eastern Europe they are setting the standards in terms of de-institutionalisation and finding family-based solutions for children in difficulty; it is the only former Communist country which has been able to dismantle effectively its vast network of child care institutions and place the children in substitute families. Although there are still major problems in Romania with corruption, and poverty, the fact that they have managed to reform their child welfare system is a huge achievement.

What is very interesting to note is that the organisations which have a financial interest in continuing international adoptions, also have a vested interest in promoting Romania as a disaster case where nothing has changed, babies continue to be abandoned, and where they are still unable to look after their own children.

Even the Romanian branch of UNICEF has taken a somewhat sensationalist angle to its work by commissioning a study which shows the rate of babies being abandoned in maternity hospitals being approximately double the official rate. This was not a case of UNICEF being right and the government being wrong; it was a case of shoddy research from which a sensational figure was announced to the press two months before the report was even written.

The fact that Romania's new law on child rights is a very good piece of legislation, better than in several EU Member States, and that Romania is one of the few countries to have found a way to de-institutionalise its children in care, has been ignored by these groups. Because of these vested interests, negative stories continue to pour out of those newspapers which do not have the resources, or interest, in finding out for themselves what the real situation is.

Getting back to the main point of this chapter, the history of international adoptions as a lesson in 'liberal democracy and globalisation', I would like to briefly describe the history of international adoptions. There has been a decline in the birth rate in several Western countries for many years. Particularly affected are the Latin countries of Italy, France and Spain. For those families who are unable to have their own children they are often presented with the opportunity of adoption; but adopting in most EU states is complicated and takes a lot of time. The procedures are complex and there are just not enough young children available for adoption. There is much more demand than supply. In the West this situation is based on the reality that child protection laws give a tight net of protection to the hundreds of thousands of EU children who are in the care of the state.

International adoption has been going on for most of this century. It started as an organised state-to-state process following the Second World War when there were thousands of displaced families, and many homeless children in Europe and Asia. It started as a genuine humanitarian action and gradually got distorted as the private companies involved got better at organising an international network, high level lobbying and Public Relations. Often, financial interests were put before the best interests of the child.

In the Islamic world and Africa the practice of international adoption is generally not allowed and until the 1990s, international adoption was not very widespread (although there were always many adoptions from South Korea to USA). This changed when the Iron Curtain fell and the economies of formerly oppressed countries began to be liberalised. During the early 1990s Romania was the country with the most international adoptions. By the end of the 1990s Russia and China were the biggest 'suppliers'. According to a recent article in the *Daily Mail* (UK) over 50,000 Chinese children have been adopted by families in the US during the last ten years[1].

The business of international adoption has grown massively since 1990. But this growth is not really subject to any set of standards and is, in effect, unregulated. As the media and public start to find out more about what goes on under the guise of international adoptions, scandals have been making the news. *The Times* of London recently published a horrifying story about the trade in child body parts from Ukraine, and suggested that international adoptions were perhaps a cover for this trade (a proper enquiry into this needs to be commissioned)[2]. There have also been some very lively debates in the Russian Parliament about the alleged murder of 15 Russian children by adoptive parents in the USA.

As the international adoption business liberalised, as a result of the opening up of the former communist countries of Eastern Europe, the business has globalised. What started out with good intentions - a family's desire to adopt; a somewhat misguided attempt to help communities in difficulty - has opened the door to less scrupulous types who have other interests than adopting a child. It concerns me greatly that the trafficking of children and body parts has burgeoned alongside the growth of illegal international adoptions.

The situation with international adoptions today is particularly interesting. Having gone from a free-for-all in the early 1990s the adoption industry has consolidated, expanded globally and now has its tentacles in scores of emerging countries around the world. This industry thrives best in economies that are in transition, where social services are undeveloped, where local officials are easily bribed, and where the international adoption process can be presented as some kind of solution. The countries that provide the highest number of adoptive

---

[1] Antonowicz, A., 'Inside China: Chinese takeaways' *Daily Mail* 9th August 2005.

[2] 'Scandal of new born babies stolen from their mothers', published in *The Times*, 10th September 2005.

children are China, Russia and some of the nations of the former Soviet Union, and a few Central American countries like Guatemala.

But regulation is catching up with the international adoption industry. Romania led the way in this regard and was always quite transparent about the problems and corruption caused by this practice. The latest scandal in Romania concerns 33 children who were adopted internationally but 'left behind' by parents who no longer wanted them. In some cases, different children were taken abroad than those who were officially approved for international adoption; in other words identities were purloined, leaving behind children who had no legal identity, no proof of existence and no access to public services. These children are now clamouring for recognition.

If we look at the history of international adoption over the last fifteen years we can see an interesting pattern, a pattern which is similar to the growth of a liberal economy in an emerging economy. This phenomenon of rapid economic growth, accompanied by a lack of regulation and the spread of corruption, is a common feature of emerging free market economies. This stage is usually followed by a first attempt to control and regulate the business, but these first attempts often fail to get things under control. Eventually the enterprise is brought under proper control even though this often means a loss of economic opportunity for some players.

Janusz Onyszkiewicz MEP and Bartek Nowak

Introduction

Since the 1999 WTO Seattle protests it has become quite common for people to accuse the international organisations of opacity and a lack of transparency. The demands of applying democratic rules of accountability and broad participation in their decision-making process brought a huge debate about democratic deficit at international level. In this context it is often assumed that the global problems can only be solved by coordinated global responses and should be controlled through traditional chains of delegation and participation. Although to some extent it is true, this attitude reflects a false premise of applying domestic democratic rules to international organisations. And it does not take into account the question of how to govern globally without having a global government.

While we consider the current model of international institutions, which has been established and developed following World War II, as - more or less - successful in terms of deepening international cooperation, it is of crucial importance to start responding to the challenges posed by the globalisation process. The difficulty is that these are challenges of tomorrow, as yet unspecified. Improving communication processes between institutions and civil society, broadening chains of participation for them and improving cooperation with national parliaments are clearly technical challenges of today, which can be implemented immediately. But technical changes, although they bring advancement, cannot be treated as the final solution.

A very fresh example is the European Union Constitutional crisis. Although a huge majority of societies consider the Constitutional Treaty a good one, they do not, in some cases, understand the complex and technical changes that it brings. In general, when talking about reform of international organisations in an era of globalisation, it is worth underlining the importance of future change on the level of paradigms. As John F. Kennedy remarkably said "Change is the law of life. And those who look only to the past or present are certain to miss the future".

In this paper we intend to briefly examine how the process of globalisation influenced activity of international institutions, what the problems and possible remedies are, and what kind of challenges the international community will have to face in the future, both on the levels of economic and security institutions. We do not pretend to propose solutions as they simply do not exist, but at least to start building the bridge for future discussions.

The pattern of globalisation

The notion of globalisation is commonly misunderstood in the public opinion. It is neither universalisation or homogenisation, nor just a liberalisation. In comparison to the beginning of the twentieth century, today's world is less globalised when taking into account restrictions in the flow of capital. The same situation occurs when we consider the migration of people; their mobility was much higher than it is today[1].

Some people very eagerly accuse globalisation of lacking human face and identify it with liberalisation pointing out the GATT/WTO undertakings and the activity of the International Monetary Fund (IMF). Despite some advancement in freeing international trade through next rounds of agreements, it is still a huge simplification. The system of international trade today is dominated not by the WTO multilateral treaties, but by the Preferential Trade Agreements and Special and Differential Treatment[2]. General lowering of customs and taxes does not mean a liberalised trade. Still, the main barriers exist not between developed and developing countries, but among developing economies. As the World Bank estimates, for developing countries more than 80% of benefits from freeing international trade would come only from lowering barriers between themselves[3]. This clearly contradicts the public image of international trade rules which are often called unfair, with the blame put on countries with developed economies.

---

[1] *Globalization, Growth and Poverty. Building an Inclusive World Economy;* The World Bank, Washington 2001.

[2] Jagdish Bhagwati calls it "spaghetti bowl". See: *The Future of the WTO. Addressing institutional challenges in the new millennium;* World Trade Organisation, Geneva 2004.

[3] *World Development Report 2003: Sustainable Development in a Dynamic World;* Oxford University Press, Washington 2003.

First of all, it is important to distinguish between globalism and globalisation. Globalism is a state of the world involving networks of interdependence at multi-continental distances[4]. It has different dimensions[5], for example, economic globalism (involving long distance flows of goods, services and capital, and the information and perceptions that accompany market exchange), military globalism (long distance networks of interdependence in which force, and the threat or promise of force, are employed), environmental globalism (the long distance transport of materials in the atmosphere or oceans or of biological substances that affect human health and well being), and social and cultural globalism (movement of ideas, information, images and of people). And "globalisation is the process by which globalism becomes increasingly thick"[6].

While there are different meanings of globalisation, we would like to underline two of them, which - we believe - are of crucial importance for activity of international institutions, and for these two factors there is a particular quest for finding solution on a global level.

First, the globalisation of new technologies. Economically, in the near future it will be a crucial factor in dividing rich and poor societies. While today the least developed countries (LDCs) suffer from a lack of basic infrastructure, it is clear that for decades they will not jump over the present technological gap. But as some predict, the future of the world's power will not be centred so much over the accessibility of information, but over the capacity to segregate relevant information from the huge volume of available data[7].

In the context of the activity of international institutions, on one side we notice the use of the new technologies which can facilitate greater

---

[4] Nye, J.S. & Donahue, J.D., (eds.), *Governance in a Globalizing World;* Brookings Institution Press, Washington D.C. 2000, p.2.

[5] Ibidem.

[6] Ibidem

[7] Toffler, A., *Powershift: Knowledge, Wealth and Violence at the edge of XXI Century;* New York, Bantam Books 1990.

democratic control by a non-defined global public opinion and strengthens the opportunities for soft influence over the decision-making process, the other side refers particularly to international institutions which are dealing with security issues.

For the international community new technologies have already created new opportunities for conducting wars or managing conflicts. But the globalisation of ICT has also caused a rapid growth of uncontrolled threats, which the international community has never before known. For global terrorist networks ICT is very helpful for preparation of their actions and for disseminating their very dangerous ideas and messages. New technologies bring also opportunities for development of new generations of weapons, which in the past no-one could ever imagine.

Secondly, we believe that in international relations following the collapse of communism, one of the greatest achievements is a slow but permanent globalisation of democratic values and norms. The spread of democratic values in the international community is in global terms real at last.

It can be very often seen that so-called global public opinion and NGO networks demand democratisation of decision-making system, broader participation, accountability and transparency of international institutions. It is quite regularly but mistakenly assumed that we should apply the same rules of democratic control and chains of participation both to national and international levels of governance. Few people remember that there is no international government, and that the international institutions cannot exist without the will of their member states, and cannot act efficiently without the agreement of each member[8]. We often notice that these institutions are frequently carried away by their own institutional dynamics which somehow drives them independently from national states. But what really matters is a general framework in which the national states still operate as the main actors. Thus, although improvement of international organisation's democratic rules is really needed in order to respond to globalisation challenges, we

---

[8] Generally speaking, in the decision-making process of international institutions the qualified majority voting system is rarely used.

should take a very balanced approach while adapting it. The globalisation of democratic values and norms, when it refers to international institutions, is also externally visible. For the last half century the sovereignty of state has remained the main paradigm of the United Nations and international law. The 60th anniversary UN summit, although it has been criticised for its modest results, brought about a very meaningful shift of the philosophy of international community[9]. There will be no more sovereignty of state as a full and unrestricted control of affairs within national borders; instead the nation state becomes obliged to protect its own citizens as well as to observe basic human rights. Such a duty raises a question about the preconditions for intervention and use of force by the international community, but it is a clear advancement which reflects the process of globalisation of democratic values.

International institutions: responding to the needs of people?

Generally speaking, the traditional model of international cooperation is based on operating through the institutions set up on a 'club model'[10]. International regimes were established by member states to govern 'issue-areas', defined in terms of clusters of issues. Cabinet ministers, or their equivalents, working in the same issue area, were gathering together to make rules and then put them into practice. They negotiated in secret, and reported their agreements to national legislatures and public. The decision making process was invisible to the public, which gave the decision makers great scope for communication manipulation.

When we take into account the efficiency in terms of the results of negotiations, the club model brought significant and often positive outcomes, albeit at a considerable price in terms of transparency and

---

[9] *2005 World Summit Outcome;* United Nations General Assembly doc A/60L.1, New York 20th September 2005.

[10] Keohane, R.O. & Nye Jr, J.S., *The Club Model of Multilateral Cooperation and the World Trade Organization: Problems of Democratic Legitimacy;* Working Paper no.4, John F. Kennedy Harvard School of Government, Cambridge MA 2004.

accountability[11]. Firstly, negotiators could produce more far-reaching compromises, as it was very difficult to hold them accountable domestically for their actions. Second, the 'issue-areas' attitude assured often very technical outputs, which could be understood by the specialists, but not by the general public.

Since the second half of the 1990s we could observe the weakening of the club model of international institutions. This was caused both by the globalisation process and a series of new challenging international events. Economically speaking, successful completion of Doha Round and launching the WTO system made the public more sensitive to further concessions in international trade. The economic crisis of South Asia and its rapid and wide spread shifted a very technical activity of the IMF to the global discourse. The first round of NATO enlargement and the accession of three post-communist countries caused a global public discussion about the world's geopolitical imperatives. The 2004 enlargement of the European Union, and the debate whether the candidate countries were internally ready for membership brought completely new challenges for Europe. While there are global challenges of a strategic nature, the slow but progressive spread of democratic values and existing fast and efficient worldwide communication system ensures that such problems cannot be solved in silence as previously. Broad public debate is needed. While it is obvious that democracies on the domestic level contain various electoral chains of influence, it is obvious that these rules are not directly applicable on the international level, at least not in the foreseeable future. But it is worthwhile pointing out, those traditional non-electoral chains of influence, as enhancement of cooperation between national parliaments and international assemblies, making national governments more transparent and accountable to public opinion with respect to their international mandate, can not be enough in order to respond to the so-called 'democratic deficit'. The last example is the case of the European Constitution. In fact it offers to hugely improve all non-electoral chains of influence of public opinion for the EU. If this treaty is implemented, the Union will surely be more democratic, more

---

[11] Bernstein, S., *The Elusive Basis of Legitimacy in Global Governance: Three Conceptions;* Working Paper of University of Toronto, May 2004.

accountable, and more transparent. It appeared that in referendums in France and the Netherlands people did not care about it. The same has also happened in the referendum with a positive outcome in Spain, as the main reasons for 'yes' votes were not related to all these improvements[12]. Perhaps it is the right time to start re-thinking some paradigms for international cooperation.

Secondly, globalisation has generated a huge proliferation of non-state agents. These are NGOs, business companies and business associations, labour unions and so on. Such a coalition, although extremely diversified, proved its ability to complicate international negotiations. In the 1999 Seattle WTO ministerial meeting they blocked the summit. During the failing Doha Round negotiations in Cancun they raised expectations of different countries so high that it appeared impossible to find any kind of consensus. Such networks learned perfectly how to use the rules of political economy, as well as on side of developing and developed countries and, paradoxically, how to use some aspects of globalisation. They use strategies that not only do not leave much scope for secret negotiations, but make compromise and concessions very difficult to be achieved. On the level of international security organisations, it is worth mentioning both the change and threat posed by the emergence of non-state actors.

Thirdly, the weakening of the club model of international institutions is caused by natural factors. We believe that international governance through issue-areas is neither eligible nor possible today. For instance, the WTO is no longer solely a trade organisation, as there is a broad spectrum of issues to be negotiated, ranging from investments, competition, intellectual and property rights to the rights of workers. The IMF demands not only the fulfilment of some monetary and fiscal goals, but demands an implementation of a broad range of macroeconomic reforms on the domestic level. NATO, since it changed its doctrine in 1999, is no longer a mere defence organisation, as it can and does go out of its area (i.e. to Kosovo and Afghanistan). Moreover, there is a big shift in understanding security threats in the contemporary world. When the NATO alliance was set up, the danger was perceived as

---

[12] See: http://www.euractiv.com/Article?tcmuri=tcm:29-130616-16&type=Overview.

'one state against another', or one bloc of states against another. Today, the threats are arising on an intra-state level, often because of weakness or a lack of state institutions[13]. In addressing the problem of internationally-organised crime or terrorism and such networks as al-Qaeda, the soft power and cooperation by international intelligence sharing and exchange of police information are of great importance. Moreover, NATO can be extremely useful for purely civilian purposes, as it has been recently demonstrated during various natural disasters. It shows simply, that the complexity of regulations and actions on the international level is so great, that in fact, agreements undertaken by the ministers of trade (WTO), finance (IMF), defence (NATO) or others, will often affect various areas of democratic governance, which is in contradiction with the prime assumptions of such institutions. It raises serious concerns, both on the level of accountability within the government, which yet can be somehow solved by improved chains of co-ordination, but - more difficult - for the accountability on the domestic and international level. This is one of the reasons for the so-called democratic deficit.

Global problems - global democratic responses?

The challenges of today's world are of a very mixed nature; therefore the responses also have to consist of a mixture of policies. Global challenges need global responses. The only actor capable of delivering such responses is the international community acting as one. In order to ensure that the actions are not undertaken chaotically or simply *ad hoc* by a coalition of the willing and capable, the nation states need a proper framework of suitable international institutions. This is how it should be, at least in theory.

The problem of today is the states which cannot modernise their structures to meet various challenges, including those resulting from globalisation. These same states blame international institutions for everything that goes wrong in domestic politics. It happens quite often that politicians do not want to see the added value of international cooperation being afraid of external constrains as well as giving a

---

[13] Fukuyama, F., *State Building: Governance and World Order in the XXI Century;* Cornell University Press, New York. 2004.

preference to alleged efficiency and prefer to act unilaterally. They see only potential losses and are not brave enough to treat these as challenges. It is a problem that all international organisations face today: the UN, NATO, EU, and the WTO.

On the other side, the dynamics of internal development of international institutions, is, to some extent, independent of the particular will of Member States, producing ever more regulations which bind the members, delivers progressively decreasing room for manoeuvre of political leadership. Too much institutionalisation causes trouble. Linking diverse countries from all over the world to the single framework is a great benefit, but flexibility, and what is in EU language called subsidiarity, are of crucial importance.

We believe that the precondition for the introduction of a new international institutional paradigm in a globalising world is finding new room for manoeuvre in political leadership. Paradoxically, for international institutions it is more probable that they will find consensus for far-reaching and brave reforms, than establish a new detailed agreement in which everybody finds something good, but nobody understands the whole concept and cannot answer simply whether the strategic aim had been achieved.

All these things mentioned above seem to be quite obvious when we examine international institutions. The EU suffers not because the Constitution is bad, but because people voted against their elites. The budget crisis also seems to be very strange. The debate is not about whether to have a modest and decentralised budget, or a big one, in which everybody has to pay more, because it operates on a very small total amount of money: approximately 1% of GDP of EU Member States. And when we examine what money is spent on the EU Common Foreign and Security Policy[14], the image of Europe being a global player disappears.

Such problems concern all the international institutions: WTO, IMF, NATO, and the UN. What it lacks is political leadership, which is seen

---

[14] More: Nowak, B., *The New Financial Perspective of the European Union 2007-2013;* Reports-Analyses 6/05, Center for International Relations, Warsaw 2005.

especially clearly in Europe. We can point out many ways of improving the legitimacy and transparency of international institutions, but even taken together these will not solve the problem. Technical change never successfully replaces adaptive challenges. All possible non-electoral improvements can and should be implemented, but leadership is indispensable.

The globalisation of democratic values and norms, and globalisation of new technologies bring the huge challenge of change. If the international institutions want to retain their legitimacy, we should start searching for some new paradigms.

Siiri Oviir MEP

Freedom of thought, speech and action have been the central concepts of liberal and political ideology since John Stuart Mill combined liberty and individuality. Democracy without liberality is impossible but liberality should not be seen to be unlimited.

It is self-evident that the free action of individuals or groups, as well as entire nations and countries, is restricted, or at least should be restricted, by the potential harm that the use of this liberty may cause to other people. Here I lay strong emphasis on the word 'potential' which means that the concept of 'liberty' involves, firstly, a future dimension. We must think in advance how our use of liberty affects others. Secondly, we must be prepared to take responsibility for our usage of liberty.

Two-way obligation

For every traditional liberal, the 'limits' of liberty means social consideration must be taken into account. Liberty and democracy in the world can be expanded only by eroding inequality. Even Mill suggested that individuality requires the protection of society. Thus, it is arguable that every individual owes something to society and it justifies the necessity to sacrifice some personal liberty to society.

It is quite probable that people who have grown up with democracy and liberalism are accustomed to such an approach to liberality. However, the people I represent have dreamed of liberty for centuries. It is easy to develop a conception that we are the masters of our own liberty now that it has triumphed and Estonia is one free country in a union of free countries.

Crumbs of equality

During the Soviet era the official opinion was that men and women were equal. However, no specific data was provided to verify this argument; in most cases those arguments remained empty. This so-called equality was often illustrated by highly-educated women in fields traditionally regarded as men's work, such as metallurgical engineering, bridge construction, and agricultural operators. The reasons for such superficial declarations were mainly ideological, the wish to present all members of Soviet society as equal. Since statistics concerning wage differences between men and women were largely undeveloped we had no clear idea of the real situation. Rather, gender differences were the concern of sociologists.

Only after Baltic countries regained independence in 1991, accompanied by a major reorganisation of statistical work, was particular importance paid to the issues of gender differences. Sociological studies were also continued which gave an insight into the long-term trends of the field. As a result of this certain issues became apparent at the beginning of the 1990s. Soviet-type 'equality' had existed only in words, in reality there were clear gender differences at the beginning of the transformation period, which deepened even further during the transformation period.

During this period of change propaganda was, to an extent, understandable. It was a reaction to the Soviet-era abstract concept of equality between men and women. It also conformed to the political approach to restoring the Estonian state along the lines of the pre-WWII model. "Women back to home!" was a slogan which became popular during the transformation period, heard in all three Baltic countries in the early 1990s. Generally speaking, the changes to gender roles in Baltic state societies could be characterised as masculine.

It should also be noted that Soviet propaganda, despite its primitive nature was actually quite effective. Even in 1993, two years after independence, more than 50% of working women thought that the same opportunities were available to them as to their male counterparts. However, by this time several important socio-political processes in Estonia had started - a transfer to a new monetary system and free-market conditions had increased unemployment. The first free elections had taken place and the different prospects of various demographic groups were becoming obvious.

Estonia has been highlighted among other ex-Soviet countries as a country of swift democratisation and successful economic reforms.

Thus one could assume that the country has experienced quicker changes, both subjectively (the level of value judgements), and objectively (the level of reality). For women it would mean improvements in gender equality in their professional lives. But is this the case? Have Estonian women, whose educational level is higher than that of Estonian men, managed to be successful for the past 15 years in developing market economy conditions? Several recent studies in the so-called Eastern bloc countries have shown that although political and economic reforms at the beginning of the 1990s caused problems adjusting for both men and women, adapting to the new situation has been somewhat more difficult for women. Women, in particular mothers with young children, but also women nearing retirement age, were, and unfortunately still are, considered society's risk groups with limited liberties.

The impact of economic reforms on employment

Radical economic reforms at the beginning of the 1990s have had differing impacts on different economic sectors. The biggest set-back occurred in the primary and secondary sectors, agriculture and industry, where production and volume diminished the most. However, at the same time the tertiary sector developed, in particular banking and service spheres. Therefore, at the beginning of the 1990s when most women were employed in the tertiary sector, and men in primary and secondary sector, more men lost their jobs due to the restructuring of the economy. Also the professional structure changed in conjunction with changes in employment structures. If the importance of men as managers, specialists and officials has continuously increased since 1992, then the share of women in this sector has thus decreased. Towards the end of the transformation period, men clearly outnumbered women among executives, top managers and leaders in society, and thus occupied a higher position on the career ladder.

Women's double workload also played a role in this. The combination of wage labour and home chores, which were largely left to women, was a tiring one. Therefore many of them - if they had the chance - opted to stay at home. 'Deficit' society was also characterised by hard living conditions which absorbed time and energy.

Competitiveness of women

Women's competitiveness proved lower than men's during the transformation period in particular but also more generally. According to Pierre Bordieu this is associated with the use of 'cultural capital'. Even after graduating from university, women's career progress becomes more erratic and insecure. Taking maternity leave sets women back several rungs on the career ladder; having children is often a considerable reason for women's career inequality.

In many cases women omit to mention their children at interview. Often, Estonian employers prefer childless candidates, usually a man, rather than a woman with a young child. Mothers are the employees excusing themselves from work due to their child's sickness; instances of fathers using children's sick-leave are a rarity in our country. The cases of fathers receiving child care benefits, based on their wage level, are very rare; men's income is, as a rule, higher and therefore the man continues to work while the woman stays at home with the young child. Also, it is usually women who take time off to care for their elderly parents because this is also considered to be a woman's responsibility.

In rural areas many childcare institutions have been closed, forcing mothers to stay at home with their children. But pre-school childcare institutions are also scarce in urban areas. These factors collectively hinder women in the workplace, making them less competitive than men.

Psychological factors

In order to evaluate the impact of economic reforms on gender equality during the transformation period we should also take into account one psychological factor. Traditionally the man is considered to be the head of the family and consequently the family's breadwinner. When there is any choice in the matter he should be guaranteed the opportunity to make a living. In times of economic hardship women are constantly portrayed as 'house fairies'.

Traditional approaches thus started to lose their importance in the first half of the 1990s, and the desire for equality increased. Women's wages gained greater importance in family finances as a result of more than just changes in 'value judgments'. Men and women became equal on the labour market.

Wage differences

Women in Eastern European economies are concentrated in low wage sectors. Wage differences are more clearly felt because men occupy more managerial positions, which naturally entail a better pay. But we cannot overlook the factor that in the 1990s there was not one role which remunerated women equally with men, even though they had equal qualifications and experience. True, some changes at the end of the 1990s took place but not all of them were in favour of women.

Recently the European Parliament presented a study of the Open Society Institute which revealed that women receive 25-30% less than their male counterparts[1]. Estonia was in the bottom three countries for gender-based wage discrepancies. Thus Estonia has a long way to go to reach the European average.

Undoubtedly, one of the reasons for such wage differences is the readiness of women to make compromises in order to suit the conditions of the job. But the price of this 'stability' has proven quite high because submissiveness makes women more vulnerable. Often the reasoning behind this is that in Estonia traditional gender stereotypes play an important part, and this is accepted not only by men but by women as well.

At the beginning of the 1990s, the overriding perception was that family was the biggest priority for women. It was even suggested that women did not wish to progress in their career or professional lives nor accept high-profile jobs because they were afraid that the associated responsibilities and heavy workload would not allow them to sufficiently commit to the family and children.

---

[1] OSI Network Women's Programme 2005. Equal Opportunities for Women and Men. www.soros.org/initiatives/women/articles_publications (accessed 18th November 2005).

Changes in value judgements

During the Estonian 'Singing Revolution' at the end of the 1980s, there was a campaign in Estonia expressed by a famous pop group 'Justament' in the song - 'The country has to be filled with children'. The ideal of the pre-war middle class family model was a woman, by the side of the head of the family, idolised only for her commitment in caring for her children and husband.

This ideal resulted in the closure of many baby nurseries and kindergartens. The woman was expected to be at home with the child for three years, and preferably until the child started school. The possibility of combining work and family life was never raised because this forced archaic family model excluded it. These questions were raised only during the second part of the 1990s as a result of EU-related debates.

The sociologists of Tallinn University International and Social Studies Institute conducted polls in 1985, 1993 and 1998 which give a good overview of the trends of the transformation period. The findings of the studies can allow us to claim that if in 1985 and 1993 the society's judgements were focused on traditional gender roles, then by 1998 certain changes had already taken place. For example, comparing the end of 1990 to 1993, the proportion of people supporting a traditional sharing of home chores changed, and the ratio of those who thought that men and women should do home tasks in equal amounts increased. The proportion of those who believed that women should do women's jobs and men should do men's jobs diminished both among men and women.

Prostitution and trafficking women

Another negative phenomenon started to spread following the regained independence of the Republic of Estonia. This is prostitution. In the Soviet Union prostitution did not officially 'exist'. During the transformation period prostitution was concealed and chaotic, but by the mid-1990s the sex industry was already well organised. From the end of the 1990s Estonia was entering international cooperation networks. International cooperation ties enabled women to be sent from Estonia to other countries. According to NGOs about 700 women a year are traded from Estonia to foreign countries as prostitutes.

It is important to emphasise that the prostitutes originate mainly from areas where the consequences of economic restructuring are the most severe. These are areas where the economy was based on raw materials from the Soviet Union, and finished products sent back in return. These regions in particular suffered from unemployment after the collapse of the Soviet Union. Economic decline was accompanied by alcohol abuse, drug addiction and AIDS.

Equality and politics

The number of women actively employed declined significantly during the transformation period. Difficulties in adapting to quick changes in society are compounded by the weakness of social organisations, and in particular by the weakness of trade unions, but also by the limited representation of women in politics. In particular women suffered under-representation in the boards of political parties, and also at the legislative and executive level. Gender equality originates from policy management and politics stems from political parties. Thus the gender equality of party politics is one of the key issues.

In societies with developing and weak democracies, politics is mainly the 'playground of men', and at least at the decision-making level there are few women in politics. For example, out of the 14 members of the Estonian government only 2 are women. The proportion of women in the Estonian Parliament - 20 women among 101 parliamentarians - puts us only at 44th position worldwide in terms of equality. Those women who have been elected to Parliament are scattered between different factions, not uniting for the cause of gender equality (at least not at the beginning of the transformation period). And since we seldom see women on the boards of parties, gender-specific issues, i.e. laws combining work and family life, do not get to the Parliament quickly enough.

Two reasons underpin the minimal roles played to date by women in politics. First, at the beginning of the transformation period their participation was inhibited by the idealisation of gender roles. Second, at the end of the transformation period and still now participation has been limited by the low credibility of political institutions. There were similar findings in both Latvia and Lithuania.

Legislative process

Debate over EU issues in the latter half of the 1990s played an important role in putting gender equality firmly on the agenda. In particular, the debates about gender equality principles in the European Social Charter and the necessity of implementing the law of gender equality in Estonia were significant in this respect.

It was only from 2000 onwards that Baltic countries put gender discrimination under legal examination. There was also no legal obligation to deal with the promotion of gender equality. Although these laws have now been adopted, as a former Minister of Social Affairs I saw first hand that the path was far from smooth. The media often raised the question about the necessity of the law on gender equality, because "it would not change anything anyway"?! The public, on the other hand, tried to deal with the main principle of human rights in a very limited manner - as a relationship between men and women.

European principles have now found a firm place in our legislation. Today, fewer people question the legislative basis. The practical implementation of these acts is rather more important: the creation of necessary structures and monitoring of the implementation of the acts. Information campaigns about European norms will play an important role in clarification at every level, in changing value judgements and introducing modern requirements for gender roles where the equality of men and women is not merely a slogan but a fundamental part of everyday life.

Liberality - shared freedom, shared obligations and equal opportunities. The globalising world needs shared liberty and equal opportunities. Years ago Timothy Garton Ash wrote an essay entitled *'Europe's Endangered Liberal Order'* the conception of which is both simple and convincing: a liberal order is the best way for Europe's development. It is undoubtedly the best way for the development of the globalising world as well. There can be no doubt: Liberal Democracy as a political movement plays a crucial role in all of this.

Karin Riis-Jørgensen MEP, Anne E. Jensen MEP and Niels Busk MEP

The first era of globalisation and global finance capitalism was shattered by the successive hammer blows of World War I, the Russian Revolution and the Great Depression, which combined to fracture the world both physically and ideologically. The divided world that emerged after World War II was then frozen in place by the Cold War. The Cold War was also an international system, lasting from 1945 to 1989, when, with the fall of the Berlin Wall, it was replaced by another system: the new era of globalisation we are now in. Call it 'Globalisation - Round II.' It turns out that the seventy-five year period from the start of World War I to the end of the Cold War was just one long 'time-out' between one era of globalisation and another.

While there are many similarities between the previous era of globalisation and this, what is new today is the degree and intensity with which the world is being tied together into a single globalised marketplace. What is also new is the sheer number of people and countries able to take part in this process and affected by it. The pre-1914 era of globalisation may have been intense, but many developing countries in that era were excluded. The pre-1914 era may have been large in scale relative to its time, but it was minuscule in absolute terms compared to today. Daily foreign exchange trading in 1900 was measured in the millions of dollars. It was $820 billion a day, according to the New York Federal Reserve. By April 1998 it was up to $1.5 trillion a day and still rising. This new era of globalisation, compared to the one before World War I, is turbocharged.

But today's era of globalisation is not only different in degree; in some very important ways it is also different in kind. As *The Economist* once noted, the previous era of globalisation was built around falling transportation costs. Thanks to the invention of the railroad, the steamship and the automobile, people could get to and trade with more places faster and more cheaply. Today's era of globalisation is built around falling telecommunications costs - of microchips, satellites, fibre optics and the Internet. According to *The Economist,* a three minute call (in 1996 dollars) between New York and London cost $300 in 1930[1]. Today it is almost free through the Internet.

New technologies are able to weave the world together even tighter. These technologies mean that developing countries don't just have to trade their raw materials to the West and get finished products in return; they mean that developing countries can become big-time producers as well. These technologies also allow companies to locate different parts of their production, research and marketing in different countries, but still tie them together through computers and teleconferencing as though they were in one place.

But shorter distances also mean greater challenges. Indeed, there is a big challenge to be met in all OECD countries that have failed to catch up with the best performers of today, in terms of GDP per capita. This is particularly notable in the case of Japan and many European economies.

Europe is falling behind

Economic 'catch up', which was widely believed to be automatic, started to stall during the 1980s and degenerated into relative decline during the 1990s. Today GDP per capita in France, Germany or Italy is 30% below US levels and, at current trends, this gap will increase during the next few years[2].

The US has a clear economic time lead, even increasing it after 2000. The current EU levels in GDP, R&D investment, productivity and employment were already reached by the US in the late seventies and early 80s. Even the most optimistic projections show it will take the EU decades to catch up and this only if there is considerable EU improvement. According to a study undertaken by Eurochambres from March 2005, the US economy is ahead of EU by at least 20 years[3]!

---

[1] 'Elementary, my dear Watson', *The Economist*, 21st September 2000. (http://www.economist.com/displayStory.cfm?Story_ID=375504).

[2] Jean-Philippe Cotis, OECD Chief Economist, March 2005.

[3] http://www.eurochambres.be/PDF/pdf_press_2005/09-SpringBusinessForum11March05.pdf.

➤ **Employment:** Europe's employment level for 2003 was achieved by the US in 1978. It will take the EU until 2023 to reach US levels of employment, and then only if EU employment growth exceeds that of the US by 0.5% p.a.

➤ **Research and Development:** Europe's R&D investment for 2002 was achieved by the US in 1979. It will take the EU until 2123 to reach US levels of R&D investment, and then only if EU investment exceeds that of the US by 0.5% p.a.

➤ **Income:** Europe's income for 2003 was achieved by the US in 1985. It will take the EU until 2072 to reach US levels of income per capita, and then only if EU income growth exceeds that of the US by 0.5% p.a.

➤ **Productivity:** Europe's level of productivity for 2003 was achieved by the US in 1989. It will take the EU until 2056 to reach US productivity rates per employed, and then only if EU productivity growth exceeds that of the US by 0.5% p.a.

The post-1995 differences in EU-US productivity patterns are fundamentally driven by the US superiority in terms of its capacity to produce and absorb new technologies, most notably in the case of ICT (Information and Communication Technology). ICT accounts for much of Europe's lag behind the US in growth performance in recent years. According to a survey by The Economist Intelligence Unit in 2004[4], ICT accounted for as much as 0.4 percentage points of the 0.52-point difference between GDP per head growth rates in the US and the Eurozone big three (Germany, France, Italy) in 1995-2002. The survey also suggested that Europe is unlikely to close this gap unless significant progress is made in areas such as skills, innovation and competition.

A wide range of factors have contributed to the US global dominance in ICT. Focused R&D activities; world class research and teaching establishments; defence procurement contracts which nurtured the ICT industry in its incubation phase in the 1950s and 1960s; and the unique combination of financing mechanisms and a highly competitive

---

[4] *The Economist Intelligence Survey 2004 - Kilde:* Reaping the benefits of ICT - Europe's productivity challenge, a report from the Economist Intelligence Unit.

domestic marketplace which brought the ICT industry from the knowledge creation phase to the critical mass market phase.

Furthermore, the US realised a long time ago that having world-class universities to produce a disproportionately large share of cutting-edge ideas and research is a prerequisite for a knowledge-based economy. And here lies another of Europe's problems. European universities have been allowed to deteriorate in quality over the past few decades.

Europe - no longer top of the class

"Universities are a mess across Europe", the Economist concluded in its September 2005 issue[5]. European countries spend only 1.1% GDP on higher education, compared with 2.7% in the United States. American universities have between two and five times as much to spend per student as European universities, which translate into smaller classes, better professors and higher-quality research.

The European Commission estimates that 400,000 EU-born scientific researchers are now working in the United States. Most have no plans to return. Europe produces only a quarter of the American number of patents per million people. It needs to ask itself not whether it can overtake the United States as the world's top knowledge economy by 2010, but how it can avoid being overtaken by China and other Asian tigers.

The basic problems with universities are the same across Europe. Governments have forced universities to educate huge armies of students on the cheap, and have deprived them of the two freedoms that they need to compete in the international marketplace: to select their students and to pay their professors the market rate for the job.

Still, Europeans are taking a couple of practical steps to improve their troubled universities. The Bologna Declaration, signed in 1999, is intended to produce a single European higher educational 'space' by introducing a combination of comparable qualifications and transferable credits. Various EU initiatives are also encouraging young people to study in other European countries. The Erasmus programme, for

---

[5] http://www.economist.com/displaystory.cfm?story_id=4340031.

example, has already benefited more than one million students. This combination of increased transparency and enhanced mobility is bound to promote competition among universities.

But this may all be too little, too late. There has been little or no progress in introducing realistic fees, freeing universities from government control or concentrating research in elite universities. Policymakers have already begun to realise that world class universities produce a disproportionately large share of cutting edge ideas and research. Look at the University of Chicago's impact on economics, and hence on economic policy. Of the 55 economists who have won the Nobel Prize since 1969, when economics was added to the roster, nine were teaching at the University of Chicago when they were awarded their prizes, and another 14 either trained at Chicago or had previously taught there.

World class universities also produce outsized economic benefits. The best known example is Stanford, which helped to incubate Google, Yahoo!, Cisco, Sun Microsystems and many other world-changing firms. The University of Texas at Austin has helped to create a high-technology cluster that employs around 100,000 people in some 1,700 companies. In 2000, the eight research universities in Boston provided a $7.4 billion boost to the region's economy, generated 264 new patents and granted 280 licenses to private enterprises.

Top universities are a valuable asset in the global battle for talent too. America's great research universities enable it to recruit more foreign PhD students than the rest of the OECD put together. The benefits of having global universities are now so evident that governments around the world are obsessed with producing 'Ivy Leagues'. The British have introduced fees in part because they want their best universities to be able to compete with the best American ones. And the British are the only ones who currently have a few universities that can match the dominant Ivy League of the US.

The EU needs to address this challenge - and fast. So far, the best attempt by the EU to step up its efforts has been the launch of the Lisbon Strategy.

The Lisbon Strategy

In March 2000 the then 15 EU leaders agreed at the Lisbon Spring Council that the EU should commit to raising the rate of growth and employment to underpin social cohesion and environmental sustainability. The US economy, building on the emergence of the so-called 'new' knowledge economy and its leadership ICTs, had begun to outperform all but the very best of the individual European economies.

The EU set itself "a strategic goal for the next decade: to become the most dynamic and competitive knowledge-based economy in the world capable of sustainable economic growth with more and better jobs and greater social cohesion, and respect for the environment"[6]. The Lisbon strategy, as it has come to be known, was a comprehensive, interdependent and self-reinforcing series of reforms.

Lisbon aims to raise private and public research and development spending as the centrepiece of a concerted effort to increase the creation and diffusion of scientific, technological and intellectual capital. It aims to foster trade and competition by completing the single market and opening up hitherto sheltered and protected sectors. It aims to improve the climate for enterprise and business. It aims to secure more flexibility and adaptability in the labor market by raising educational and skill levels, pursuing active labor market policies, and encouraging that Europe's welfare states help the growth of employment and productivity rather than hinder it. And it aims for growth to be environmentally sustainable.

The arguments supporting that strategy are no less compelling today - maybe even more so. However, as the report 'Facing the Challenges'[7] by the High Level Group chaired by Wim Kok emphasised, Lisbon should be understood as a means of transitioning the European economy, from structures in which it essentially caught up with the

---

[6] Kilde, Lisbon European Council 23rd and 24th March 2000, Presidency Conclusions(http://www.europarl.eu.int/summits/lis1_en.htm).

[7] 'Facing the Challenge - The Lisbon strategy for growth and employment', report from the High Level Group chaired by Wim Kok, November 2004. (http://europa.eu.int/growthandjobs/pdf/kok_report_en.pdf).

world's best, to establishing economic structures that will allow it to exercise economic leadership.

The Lisbon Strategy is well meant. However, because of the range of its ambition, it covers a number of areas in which the EU has no constitutional competence and which were the preserve of Member States. At Lisbon and at subsequent spring European Councils a series of ambitious targets were established to support the development of a world-beating European economy. But halfway to 2010 the overall picture is very mixed and much needs to be done in order to prevent Lisbon from becoming a synonym for missed objectives and failed promises.

European enlargement, while welcome, has made European-wide achievement of the Lisbon goals even harder. The new Member States tend to have much lower employment rates and productivity levels; achieving the R&D goals, for example, from a lower base is even tougher than for the original EU-15 who signed Lisbon.

What should the EU do? - Keep it simple

Globalisation presents an opportunity for everyone. Globalisation is not a threat. Globalisation is a chance. If tackled positively, globalisation can benefit the vast majority of our citizens. A defensive strategy, on the other hand, will require endless protection of industries and businesses that are clearly not competitive. And yes, in the short term, it might work. But I cannot see how this will enable Europeans to compete globally in the long run. In the end, such a strategy will not save one single job in Europe.

Reaping the full benefits of a creative, positive strategy towards globalisation requires two things. First, we must carry out the necessary reforms to prepare our societies for the challenges of the future and second we must work to liberalise trade through free and open markets.

The EU needs to shift the emphasis in its present economic model more towards innovation, higher education and investment in R&D. This shift is necessitated by the increasing competitive pressures of globalisation, by the future challenges of ageing populations and by the fact that many of the EU's Member States are close to the technology frontier.

Many countries in the developed world have recognised the seismic nature of the change and are responding positively by embracing an open-economy, innovation-based model which emphasises the importance of world class educational establishments; higher levels of excellence driven and better targeted R&D; more market-based financing systems; and more flexible regulatory and institutional frameworks delivering a more dynamic and competitive business environment.

Others are responding in an inappropriate manner by attempting to cling to the belief that our present economic problems are temporary and that the magnitude of the changes wrought by globalisation will avoid the need for fundamental reforms. In this context, the collective challenge for EU governments is to embrace the reality of a rapidly changing global marketplace and of the structural changes which it inevitably provokes. While Lisbon is a manifestation of this collective desire for change, implementation of the needed reforms will be the ultimate test of whether the future will bring a substantial improvement in the EU's productivity fortunes or confirm the EU's ongoing decline as a global economic power.

Without an acceptance of the need for excellence in education and research; more appropriate market conditions aimed at delivering a more dynamic and competitive environment; and the ambition to be world leaders in specific high-tech industries; a Lisbon-induced shift of resources into knowledge production activities will have little impact on bridging the gap between the EU and the US. The success of such a scheme is determined not only by the amount of financial resources devoted to knowledge production but more importantly by an acceptance of the need to radically improve the linkages in the innovation system and to make painful changes in many of the EU's economic and regulatory environment.

István Szent-Iványi MEP

At the beginning of the eighties, when I began my political career as a dissenting university student before joining the opposition, the word 'globalisation' had yet to enter modern-day political jargon. No wonder. At that time, the inhabitants of our globe lived in three strictly separated worlds. The relationship between the First and Second Worlds was based on distrust or even open hostility. As one of the dissident subjects of the Second World, I could only hope - to be honest, without much expectation - that the division of our planet would end in a reasonably short period of time.

The Iron Curtain between the First and Second Worlds served as a front line of the Cold War. There was an unrelenting rivalry for land, water, air and space that manifested itself into, among others, an arms race, but equally affected all walks of life: science, culture and even sports, threatening to devastate our globe. Sadly enough, it was the Third World that fell victim to the fight between the two blocs. It has been destroyed by proxy wars, suffered enormously under the ruthless reign of its dictators, often the clients of one of the two worlds. Convergence theories started to surface as early as the 1960s, including the first and widely acclaimed report by the Club of Rome in 1972, which directed our attention to the emerging global challenges. Despite this it would still have been premature to speak of globalisation at a time when the three communities coexisted on the basis of being separate from each other.

It is not by coincidence that the fall of communism and the disintegration of the Second World have brought about a golden age of discourse on globalisation. However, globalisation has been the cause as well as the product of the changes since 1989. This point might require some explanation as in the previous paragraph I argued that there is little sense in discussing globalisation prior to 1989, and now I am claiming that it has been one of the root causes of the *annus mirabilis.* In fact, there is no contradiction between the two statements. In my opinion, the origins of globalisation can be traced back to the years following World War II. I am aware that some are prepared to go even further back, and link the beginnings of globalisation to the birth of global commerce. Still, I regard World War II as a dividing line with the creation of the United Nations and its specialised agencies, including the Bretton Woods institutions. This signalled a genuine shift towards a world economy and highlighted the constantly growing economic interdependence between the three worlds.

The worldwide spread of radio and television made it possible - of course, mainly for the people of the First World - to follow the most important events just as they were happening. But even in the Second World, the proliferation of short wave radio receivers broke the monopoly of information. As I am writing this, memories of my father jump to mind: he would hide in our bathroom to listen to Radio Free Europe or the Hungarian programme on the BBC in complete privacy, shutting out unwanted ears and preventing unpleasant inquiries. Hundreds of thousands of fellow subjects did the same across the Second World to obtain vital information on the current state of affairs. Often this was the only reliable news source for the Soviet bloc as well.

The flow of information undoubtedly played an important role in the collapse of dictatorships throughout Central and Eastern Europe. The debate is still far from over as regards the causes of this phenomenon, and it is very likely that it might never reach a conclusion. Some attribute the success of the First World to President Reagan's ambitious Star Wars programme that the Soviet Union was unable to catch up with, while others attach greater significance to Mr Gorbachev's reform efforts. There are also voices that impute the changes to the activities of the 'Solidarnosc' in Poland and other opposition movements in the region. There is an element of truth in all these observations. However, at the end of the day, it is equally true that the communist regimes simply could not compete with the First World any more. Their inability to do so has been largely the result of the effects of globalisation.

As long as the Eastern bloc managed to maintain its isolation based on a self-sufficient economy, it could remain unaffected by the pressures of competition. This was the case in Stalin's Soviet Union, Mao Zedong's China, and, to a lesser extent, in Enver Hoxha's Albania. But when these countries decided to engage in the world economy in order to preserve their military might, they could no longer cover up the structural weaknesses inherent in the communist system. Gorbachev or Deng Xiaoping drew the inevitable conclusions from the situation. If the communist empires had been without economic or ideological rivals or the existence of these rivals could have been denied or ignored, such monstrous entities would exist even today. Fortunately, globalisation made such a course through history impossible.

In addition to economic factors, there is another, often underestimated, aspect to the fall of communism connected to globalisation. As the decline of the communist system became obvious, as its ideology gradually lost appeal, the vacuum began to be filled by a longing for the symbolic consumer goods of the West. The mass products and consumer habits that have become commonplace in the First World since the 1950s, had enormous impact on our societies, and affected many of the developing countries. Literally millions of people wanted to wear jeans and baseball caps, drink Coca-Cola, eat a hamburger at McDonald's, listen to the music of world-famous pop stars, and watch Hollywood movies. It was a way of protest against the circumstances we were forced to live in, and the dictatorships couldn't do anything to effectively oppress such manifestations.

Of course, Coca-Cola was banned for some time, wearing hair long or jeans were also prohibited in several institutions, popular Western bands weren't allowed to perform live and their records were not even circulated or broadcast. Yet precisely because of the ever-strengthening globalisation, the process could not be reversed. As a member of the former opposition, I must admit that Western popular culture played a far greater role in the erosion of the Eastern bloc than the underground leaflets and brochures we produced and distributed. I remain convinced that the hatred of the fundamentalists in the Middle East and in other parts of the world directed against the West is at least partly due to their inability to control the expansion of our popular culture and consumer products.

Furthermore, political analysts confirm the effect of globalisation in the collapse of dictatorships and authoritarian regimes in Latin America and the start of the democratic process in some Asian countries. The very fact that events happening thousands of miles apart may have an impact on each other cannot be explained otherwise. The winds of change blowing from Central and Eastern Europe were felt in Beijing, transformed Mongolia, and accelerated democratisation in South Korea and Taiwan. The participants of these historic processes felt solidarity for each other, and followed developments in remote corners of the world with great enthusiasm and empathy.

It is not surprising that these events have inspired Francis Fukuyama, one of the most fashionable political analysts of the age, to conclude the end of history and irreversible triumph of liberal democracies. Between 1989 and 1991, almost every month we could witness the birth of a new democracy, a trend that at the time seemed universal. Since then, we know that, unfortunately, this was not the case, and today the number of stable democracies does not substantially exceed that in 1991. The enemies of open society are much more resilient than one could ever have imagined.

Nevertheless, I am optimistic. Without trying to endow globalisation with characteristics or virtues it doesn't possess, I am confident that finally it will bring down contemporary closed societies. All we have to do is take a look at the amazing evolution of communication technology from traditional television through satellites to broadband internet. The existing IT infrastructure provides us the opportunity of real time communication worldwide. It is only natural that dictators are using all tools at their disposal to monitor or restrict these communication facilities.

However, it is increasingly clear that they have lost this struggle and that their monopoly of information has ended for good. In China, hundreds of millions surf on the internet every day, and their example is followed by millions in Iran. Since local authorities are unable to exert real control, a Chinese internet user now has the luxury to choose between 4 million domestic web sites and blogs, in addition to international options. The number of critical or outright opposition blogs is constantly growing, and in place of every deleted or suppressed blog, ten new ones are created. Citizens are now able to chat, exchange information, and protest through the internet, and the time will come when they will use this tool to organise themselves. As a former opposition activist, I envy the possibilities modern technology has to offer for dissenters.

Opening borders, demolishing barriers and letting in new ideas naturally makes people feel insecure and anxious. It is also true that the process of globalisation has had very diverse effects in different parts of our world, and its benevolent corollaries are far from being justly distributed. However, it has become self-evident by now - at least among Liberals and Democrats - that our main task at the moment is not to engage in an irrational and meaningless fight against globalisation, but to make the most of it for all of us. It is apparent that the only way to do this is through the promotion of regional integration and global governance, instead of holding on to the idea of national sovereignty which past decades have revealed to be little more than a fiction. The successful management of globalisation requires adequate mechanisms that surpass those of traditional bilateral relations or international organisations. Liberals and Democrats have always been the advocates of a supranational approach in areas where it would bring an added value to existing structures. It's time to match global challenges with global answers.

Globalisation is not a phenomenon we must love or hate. It is neither the single cause nor a magical cure-all for the diseases of modern society, just a simple fact of life we have to face. It is good to know, though, that it appears to favour those who strive for freedom.

Graham Watson MEP

In the twenty-first century of the Gregorian calendar humankind enjoys greater opportunity and suffers greater misery than in any previous hundred-year period. The gap between the 'haves' and the 'have nots' is wider than at almost any previous point in history. Our understanding of the planet we inhabit, of the universe to which it belongs and the characteristics of life on earth is more comprehensive than ever. Yet the uses to which our knowledge and resources are put are rarely inspired by altruism or a sense of the common good. Liberals and Democrats believe there are serious imbalances in our world which are capable of correction to provide greater security, prosperity and opportunity - and lead thereby to greater happiness and fulfilment - for all humankind.

This essay looks at the major challenges of globalisation from a Liberal Democratic political perspective and sketches the outlines of the policies needed to meet them.

The first challenge is to stabilise the population of the planet, which has risen from 545 million people in 1600 to 2,400 million in 1950 and over 6 billion in 2005. In societies which have achieved greater levels of wealth and security, population numbers are in decline. There appears to be almost a direct correlation between levels of wealth and childbirth. Niger has the highest birth rate in the world (48.91 births/1,000 population) and Germany the lowest at 8.45[1]. Since population growth puts a strain on the earth's natural resources which the planet does not have a limitless capacity to bear it is imperative to bring all societies up to a level of wealth at which population levels will stabilise. Alternative ways to restrict population growth - forced sterilisation, or government-imposed limits on childbirth such as those in force in China - are not acceptable to Liberal Democrats.

Inequality in levels of security, wealth and opportunity also spurs population movement. In good circumstances, only a tiny fraction of members of a society will seek to emigrate to a new life elsewhere. In

---

[1] www.aneki.com (accessed 8th June 2005).

difficult times, when countries are ravaged by war or disease or environmental degradation, the percentage will increase. Large scale emigration took place in the fifteenth century when the fall of the Byzantine Empire to the Chinese triggered a mass exodus of people seeking to avoid foreign domination. More recently economic hardship and the slow speed of reform in Moldova in the past decade has resulted in an estimated loss of 30% of the active population. It should be an aim of public policy to provide conditions in which families and communities can remain united, though interaction between different communities and the development of mutual knowledge and understanding bring huge gains and should be encouraged.

The second challenge is peace. Life on earth is too often scarred by human strife, of which the causes are many. Competition for natural resources or for access to markets frequently lies at the root of war. Intolerance between people of different religion or race breeds conflict, as does resentment about the influence of one civilisation over another. The parts of the world where the three major monotheistic religions meet - Islam, Christianity and Judaism - are well-known hotbeds of conflict. But conflict between 'fundamental' religious believers and those of a secular disposition is also on the rise.

Ideological totalitarianism, too, has been a major source of strife. Though democracy is still spreading, the world's major authoritarian regimes (China and Russia) and its many minor ones (notably Saudi Arabia, North Korea, Burma, Cuba, and most of the central Asian republics) are regular offenders against modern standards of human decency. Mature democracies which should lead by example, such as the USA, have recently allowed their standards of respect for human rights to slip, for example in Guantanamo Bay and in detention centres in Afganistan and Iraq, thereby giving moral free rein to the world's more persistent offenders. Liberal Democrats remain convinced that policies against terrorism should respect fully the provisions of the Geneva conventions and the international declaration of human rights.

The US-UK led invasion of Iraq without UN support is an affront to democracy and global solidarity. The current occupation fans the flames of radical Islam. Yet modern war is more often within than between states. The horrors of conflict in the Democratic Republic of the Congo or in Darfur in Sudan require new public policy approaches. Liberals and Democrats are deeply concerned at the indifference displayed by the international community and the inability of the United Nations to prevent mass rape and murder in Darfur and elsewhere. UN Security Council members should commit themselves not to use the veto in dealing with genocide, crimes against humanity and war crimes. The conclusions of the UN summit of September 2005, though disappointing in other respects, offer hope in this area.

A Liberal Democrat response to conflict prevention starts with action against the manufacture of and trade in weapons. Easy availability of weaponry and munitions increases violence, prolongs wars and enables widespread human rights abuses. Amnesty International argues that the majority of current armed conflicts could not be sustained without the supply of small arms and light weapons and associated munition. They point out that in Columbia, arms have been supplied by the USA, Brazil, France, Germany, Spain, South Africa, the Czech Republic and Italy[2]. Liberal Democrats have pressed for an international treaty to control the trade in small arms, which are used to kill half a million people every year.

Bringing to justice those guilty of war crimes is also a must for Liberal Democrats. The development of the International Criminal Court in The Hague has been a major step forward for us in this regard.

A deeply worrying development in capacity for warfare lies in the development of weapons in space. Low orbit space is less than 150km distant from the earth, providing a country possessing the technology to launch weapons from space with a considerable proximity to any target. The USA will spend about $3bn in 2005 on space control and space force projection programmes, including anti-satellite and space-based missile launch capabilities[3]. The dangers of other major powers being

---

[2] Amnesty International Annual Report, 2004.

[3] Lewis, J., www.armscontrol.org. (Accessed 8th June 2005).

pulled into an arms race in space and of a superpower conflict involving destruction of satellites are very real. The United States Space Command's 'Vision for 2020' argues that "space superiority is emerging as an essential element of battlefield success and future warfare" and identifies 'control of space' as one of its operational concepts.

Liberal Democrats believe there is an urgent need to update the 1967 Outer Space Treaty, which calls for the use of space to be conducted "for the benefit and in the interests of all countries". The US-USSR Incidents at Sea Accord (INCSEA) of 1972, which has served as a model for comparable agreements signed by more than thirty other seafaring nations, might be used as a basis for a new treaty for spacefaring nations which should also contain 'rules of the road' to help prevent dangerous military activities leading to incidents of conflict. It would include provisions against simulated attacks, the testing and deployment of space weapons and dangerous manoeuvres in space.

Safeguarding the natural environment is a third major challenge, and arguably the most important of all. Water, air and soil are all under threat.

Water is the key to all animal and plant life. There are 263 transboundary rivers and lakes in the world. The importance of agreement on the use of the water they carry is immense. Air and soil too are shared resources, vital to life. Pollution of either is known to have serious adverse effects on human health. Yet the industrialised world, despite recent agreements to limit emissions, pumps 20m tonnes of carbon dioxide into the air and 4.5 billion litres of chemical fertiliser into the soil every year. This causes degradation of air quality and eutrophication of water, both impacting on the ability of our planet to sustain life.

The ozone layer, which protects the earth from the harmful rays of the sun, is thinning as a result of human activity, particularly the burning of fossil fuels. The hole in the layer which has opened up over Antarctica is causing skin cancer in humans and blindness in some other animals.

Urgent concerted action is necessary to stop - and, if possible, reverse - this destruction of ozone. Despite the capacity of the world's oceans to absorb increases in world temperature, CO2 emissions and other greenhouse gases are almost certainly changing climate patterns too, changing the shape and extent of the heat belt known as 'El Niño' which determines temperatures in the summer months over much of the equatorial latitudes. 1998 was the warmest year in the past 2000 years, and the decade from 1990 to 2000 proved to be the warmest decade. Professor Ralph Keeling of the University of California argues that if humankind had acted on the Cherney Report of the late 1970s we could have prevented the concentration of CO2 in the atmosphere causing climate change; it is now too late, but we may still be able to control the pace of climate change and therefore limit the damage caused by shrinking ice caps and rising sea levels.

Liberal Democrats believe that in addition to the market mechanisms agreed under the Kyoto Protocol to stabilise CO2 emissions, government action must be taken to limit global warming to 2 degrees centigrade and to limit CO2 concentration to 550 ppm. This will require environmental incentives to reduce carbon intensity, technology enabled breakthroughs to cut energy use and a mandatory cap on carbon emissions. The idea of the 'stability triangle' developed by Christopher Mottershead of British Petroleum to keep carbon emissions to their year 2000 level until 2050 offers a useful framework for public policy.

With the world's population forecast to grow by 50% by 2050, a partnership between developed and developing countries will be essential: the former must cut carbon and nitrogen emissions, the latter must develop cleanly and manage carefully the use of coal. Co-production of food and fuel (i.e. developing biofuels as a co-product of food production through the use of enzymes to break down crop waste) will also be important. In every area of human activity, the precautionary principle must guide Liberal Democrats and advise policies designed to improve our stewardship of the natural environment.

Education (especially of women) lies at the heart of Liberal Democrat strategy to resolve and prevent conflict and to safeguard the environment. Better educated people are less easily misled. Formal education of all children is important; currently 120 million children worldwide are receiving no formal education. But girls are currently less likely to be chosen by their parents to attend school than boys, even though women provide better social glue and social support systems than men and are more important determinants of human behaviour.

Beyond formal education, education in civil society is also needed. In this area, the work of the Soros Foundation, the National Endowment for Democracy and the European political foundations such as those in Germany are examples of good practice. Where once people in Europe or North America spoke of a North-South or an East-West conflict, a broader understanding of the complexity of conflict and the imperative for co habitation is growing and with it a recognition of the value of democracy and good governance which favours cohabitation.

Though huge progress has been made in medical science in the past quarter millennium, millions of people still die of or are crippled by preventable diseases. With good health so important as a factor of human happiness, improving human health is a challenge Liberal Democrats cannot ignore.

The failure of humankind to prevent the spread of the HIV/AIDS virus, which is ravaging whole populations, is awesome in its terrible implications. During 2003, young people aged 15-24 years accounted for half of all new HIV infections worldwide; more than 6,000 became infected with HIV every day[4]. For the developed world to pay so little attention to HIV, AIDS and other diseases suggests a degree of cynicism sadly at odds with the social solidarity which Liberal Democrats hold to be essential. For some churches to condemn the use of condoms, which could save the lives of thousands, is little short of criminal neglect.

The World Health Organisation must be mobilised to focus global energies in the fight against AIDS. The WHO lobbies national

---

[4] http://www.avert.org/worldstats.htm.

governments to increase access to treatments and efforts aimed at prevention. It principally provides care and support in the community with a view to preventing mother-child transmission. Governments must also put pressure on pharmaceutical companies to make available at affordable prices drugs used in treating those infected with the HIV virus.

TB, ebola, malaria and avian flu are other diseases which pose the risk of becoming epidemic. Though it does not yet transmit easily to human beings, the HN51 strain of avian flu is becoming a serious threat to bird populations as 2005 draws to a close. Greater cooperation between governments, including the sharing of information and the common development of prevention strategies, must be a priority.

The plight of women is a challenge which can no longer be underestimated. Women are victims of genital mutilation, violence and rape on an unprecedented scale. Honour killings persist in many Islamic countries. Rape is used as a tool of repression by government troops in Burma. As a weapon of war it is widespread in Africa. Discrimination against women persists even in developed countries. The work of Emma Bonino MEP and others in raising awareness of women's rights and in building mutual support groups to empower women to stand up against discrimination is a shining example of Liberal Democratic ideas in practice.

Internationally-organised crime poses perhaps the most immediate threat to people's security. Criminal syndicates built around the growing and processing of narcotic drugs in countries like Colombia or Afghanistan, involved in the smuggling of small arms and of weapons-grade fissile nuclear material stolen from poorly guarded small nuclear reactors in the Commonwealth of Independent States[5], profiting too from the vile trade in human beings for the purpose of sexual or other forms of exploitation and increasingly linked to terrorists - since they need terrorists to keep countries like Colombia or Afghanistan ungovernable - pose a massive threat to individual liberty.

---

[5] In 1994 there were five known cases of weapons materials smuggled into Europe from Russia and former Soviet Republics. There have been numerous unsubstantiated incidences since.

Terrorism poses perhaps the most visible current threat to human freedom. As Gijs de Vries, the EU's Counter-Terrorism Coordinator (and a predecessor of mine as Leader of the Liberals and Democrats in the European Parliament) has pointed out, terrorists attack fundamental human rights: the right to life, the right to a life lived in freedom from fear. They attack the essence of democracy, which is that political differences are settled through rational deliberation and the power of law instead of by the bullet and the bomb[6].

To fight internationally-organised crime, including the international terrorism which has caused recent outrages in New York, Istanbul, Madrid, London, Bali and elsewhere, cooperation between democratic governments must be extended hugely. The sharing of criminal intelligence information, cooperation between police forces and judiciaries and cross-border tracking of criminal communications and money movement are essential. Those who oppose or seek to retard such cooperation are promoting international anarchy, often in the name of national sovereignty.

The trafficking of drugs and people are significant causes of human misery. Strategies to combat these crimes in developed countries have focused on hitting supply and have not been effective. Liberals and Democrats are increasingly of the view that focusing on cutting demand would produce greater benefits at lower cost, both in financial terms and in terms of interference with human freedom.

Opening markets is another great challenge for Liberals and Democrats. It must be accompanied by safeguards, however, for those who benefit from open markets are not only the law-abiders. Illegitimate trade probably accounts for between two and six percent of global GDP; that is, between EUR 492bn and EUR 1.25trn[7]. While legitimate trade in goods or services brings mutual enrichment and furthers human understanding and peaceful relations, illegitimate trade destroys

---

[6] Gijs de Vries, European Counter-Terrorism Coordinator. Speech to Liberal International Conference, Sofia, May 13th 2004.

[7] www.wto.org. (Accessed 8th June 2005).

communities (through the environmental devastation of logging or the social devastation of drug-related crime) in the country of origin just as much as in the country of destination. Never has the need been greater for supranational measures to tackle the supranational challenge of policing trade.

The power of legitimate trade is perhaps only now being fully appreciated. The value of world trade has grown from EUR 48bn in 1948 to EUR 6.04trn by 2003. In Asia, it has lifted 600 million people over the poverty line in the space of a single generation.

Nonetheless, the economic dynamism of countries like India and China which enjoy the world's highest economic growth rates obscures the fate of the 14 Asia and Pacific countries which rank among the poorest of the world's poor. Nearly 450 million people in countries from Afghanistan and Bangladesh to the tiny pacific island of Tuvalu live on less than a quarter of the average income of the rest of the region. Yet none of these countries is eligible for relief under the HIPC initiative and they receive in total less than half of the world's development aid though they house two-thirds of its poor. While the current Western focus on poverty in Africa is laudable, it ignores a huge challenge in Asia.

Liberals and Democrats should encourage the faster-developing countries to cycle their budget surpluses into further development rather than into US$ or euro denominated investments. The current account balances of developing and emerging market nations swung from a deficit of $88bn in 1996 to a surplus of $336bn in 2004. In the same period the US current account deficit grew from $120bn to $666bn, financed mainly by borrowing from these countries. After a series of financial crises from 1996 to 2002 which caused painful devaluations and sharp economic contractions, developing countries boosted exports and restricted imports to protect themselves against future capital flight, through the accumulation of foreign currency reserves. In 2004, the reserves of developing countries grew by $400bn[8]. Such accumulation of reserves makes good monetary sense but deprives the poor of the chance to develop.

---

[8] Figures from the Institute of International Finance.

Another current challenge is how to ensure that free trade is also fair trade. Not even Liberal Democrats could deny that freer trade sometimes harms the poor. Trade in services, in particular, would benefit from a greater recognition that there is a legitimate role for state regulation where the gains from remedying market failure - for people or for the environment - outweigh the cost of government intervention. Agreement within the WTO and elsewhere on which services constitute services of general interest would be highly desirable in this regard.

Perhaps the biggest factor of change in human development has been the advances made in communications science. The establishment of the Internet in 1965 by Tim Berners-Lee et al, and developments in satellite and mobile telephone communication have changed and continue to change the framework for human interaction. The development of the Voice Over Internet Protocol (VOIP) is cutting the cost of verbal exchanges just as the world wide web brings the printed word to so many more so much more quickly. Televisual image transmission brings the world to our living rooms. This in itself poses new challenges. While such advances in communication vastly expand the access of people to knowledge and information and improve immeasurably opportunities to share ideas (and allow investment to move more quickly to the most profitable places), they are not free from interference by governments which seek to deny to their own people the fruits of such progress. Moreover, use of electronic technology for the purposes of eavesdropping or control by government of the activities of individuals has expanded at an alarming rate and at potentially great cost to human freedom. Freedom of information and strict laws on privacy and data protection therefore remain priority areas for Liberal Democrats.

The challenges posed by globalisation and discussed above are by their nature supranational, while humankind is organised mainly into nation states. The European Union has been a largely successful experiment in supranational government, though it has yet to win over the hearts of its citizens. The United Nations is in the midst of a major reflection about its raison d'être. Needing to move from the role of a passive referee to one of an operational force, it finds it lacks the management structure and the political commitment from its member nations to give it the resources and tools to do the job. Its successes in Burundi and Sierra Leone are offset by its failure in Darfur and elsewhere. Embarrassing disclosures about its management have further soured relations with its largest funder. Renewed political commitment from its members, combined with major internal reform, is urgently needed.

Unlike the right wing in politics, Liberal Democrats have no ideological difficulty with the development of supranational responses to the supranational challenges of our age; indeed, national ideologies are threatened by Liberalism less because of the size of its political presence than because of the strength of its ideas. Socialism appears to have lost its way not only because it lacks maps of the new country which it is crossing, but because it thinks maps are unnecessary for experienced travellers[9]. And among the many features of green parties which we find unattractive is their resistance to scientific and technological progress.

Liberal Democrats are the world's hope-mongers. We are not naïve about human nature, but we are inspired by the capacity of the human spirit for altruism and solidarity. Our growing political success beyond Europe and North America is testimony to the global appeal of our ideas, which can be found historically in Islamic and Buddhist thought, not just in the West[10]. We believe, with Victor Hugo, that the day will come when the only battlefields will be those of markets open for business and the human spirit open for ideas. We share the optimism of the Irish poet Seamus Heaney that we might look forward 'to a time when hope and history will rhyme'. We work to those ends.

WESTMINSTER KINGSWAY COLLEGE
KINGS CROSS LEARNING CENTRE

---

[9] This observation was first made by British Labour politician Richard Crossman.

[10] Sen, A., 'The diverse ancestry of democracy', Financial Times 13th June 2005.